VALUES AND ETHICS IN SOCIAL WORK

2nd Edition

VALUES AND ETHICS IN SOCIAL WORK

CHRIS BECKETT AND ANDREW MAYNARD

Los Angeles | London | New Delhi
Singapore | Washington DC

Los Angeles | London | New Delhi
Singapore | Washington DC

SAGE Publications Ltd
1 Oliver's Yard
55 City Road
London EC1Y 1SP

SAGE Publications Inc.
2455 Teller Road
Thousand Oaks, California 91320

SAGE Publications India Pvt Ltd
B 1/I 1 Mohan Cooperative Industrial Area
Mathura Road
New Delhi 110 044

SAGE Publications Asia-Pacific Pte Ltd
3 Church Street
#10-04 Samsung Hub
Singapore 049483

Editor: Sarah Gibson
Assistant editor: Emma Milman
Production editor: Katie Forsythe
Copyeditor: Sharon Cawood
Proofreader: Kate Wood
Marketing manager: Tamara Navaratnam
Cover design: Wendy Scott
Typeset by: C&M Digitals (P) Ltd, Chennai, India
Printed by CPI Group (UK) Ltd, Croydon, CR0 4YY

Library of Congress Control Number: 2012934054

British Library Cataloguing in Publication data

A catalogue record for this book is available from the British Library

ISBN 978-1-4462-0319-4
ISBN 978-1-4462-0320-0 (pbk)

Chris would like to dedicate this book to his father, Philip Beckett, with much love.

CONTENTS

DETAILED CONTENTS

LIST OF EXERCISES

LIST OF FIGURES

ABOUT THE AUTHORS

Chris Beckett completed his first degree in psychology at Bristol University before qualifying as a social worker in Bangor, North Wales. He worked for eight years as a generic social worker in a field work team, and was then a social work manager for ten years, latterly the manager of a children and families' social work team. Chris then became a lecturer in social work, working for ten years at Anglia Ruskin University in Cambridge before moving to his current post at the University of East Anglia in Norwich. He has a parallel career as a writer of fiction. Chris's short story collection, *The Turing Test*, won the Edge Hill Short Fiction award in 2009, beating collections by previous winners of the Booker and Whitbread prizes. His latest novel, *Dark Eden*, was published by Corvus in January 2012.

Andrew Maynard is a qualified social worker with many years experience in the field of child care, child protection, and fostering and adoption. He worked as a senior practitioner and a team leader in the field of child protection and has a keen interest in family therapy. He has also worked as a consultant/trainer specialising in the area of child care, child protection, diversity, race awareness and equal opportunities. Andrew currently works at Anglia Ruskin University as a principal lecturer and is the programme leader for the social work course there.

COMPANION WEBSITE

As a purchaser of this book you can access a Companion Website to be used along-side this book. This consists of a number of 5–10 minute videos of authors Chris and Andrew discussing the issues covered in each chapter of the book. These short clips will aid and enhance your understanding of the importance of values and ethics in each area of social work. The videos also give a unique insight into the authors' own values and ethics base and reveal why they decided to write and update *Values and Ethics in Social Work*.

Visit www.sagepub.co.uk/beckettandmaynard to view the relevant material.

PREFACE TO THE SECOND EDITION

The revisions to this second edition of *Values and Ethics in Social Work* reflect developments in our own thinking, as well as our responses to constructive feedback on the first edition from various sources, for which we are very grateful. The book has been re-organised somewhat. It is now in two parts instead of three, the chapter order has been revised and we have added two new chapters: Chapter 4 ('Values and politics', which includes some material that had previously appeared in the chapter on power) and Chapter 5 ('Realism as an ethical principle', which incorporates some material that had previously been included in the chapter on resources). Many of the remaining chapters have been very substantially re-written, while some have been more lightly revised. Throughout, we have added references to recent literature, and sometimes to recent events in the news. We would like to think that the end result is not just an updated text, but a revitalised and improved one. We hope that the reader will agree.

INTRODUCTION

Social work is a profession that engages with some of the most vulnerable, disempowered and discriminated-against members of society, people who often struggle to have their voice heard and listened to. The purpose of social work is to try and address some of this disadvantage, but social work itself is very powerful in relation to many of the people that it works with, and can easily be oppressive in itself, even with the best of intentions. It has the capacity to make things better, certainly, but also the capacity to make things worse. Obviously, we want to do the former, and try, as far as we possibly can, to avoid the latter, but there is no simple rule for getting it right, no formula that can be unthinkingly applied to ensure that things always come out for the best. Social workers who genuinely wish to do the right thing by their service users have no alternative but to constantly think and rethink the principles and assumptions which form the basis of their actions.

This book sets out to help social work students begin to explore the kinds of moral questions that they will encounter in practice. We have tried throughout to give at least a sense of the complexity of the real-life situations that social workers encounter, and of the difficulty of applying ethical principles when these principles often pull us in many different directions. And we have tried too to avoid giving the impression that the values and ethical principles necessary for doing social work well can be encapsulated by a series of noble-sounding words, or noble-sounding aspirations. Ethical practice, in our view, is hard work.

The book is set out in two parts. Part I ('Foundations of Values and Ethics') deals with broad ideas about values and ethics in general, looking at philosophy, religion and politics, as well as at what we call 'the duty of realism': the need to ground your thinking in what is actually there, rather than on what you might wish or like to be there. Part II ('Values and Ethics in Practice') takes the discussion into a number of different areas which are particularly relevant to social work: the meaning of professionalism, the use and misuse of power, the idea of self-determination, the contrast between oppression and respect, the ethical problems that arise when working with finite resources, and the challenges of working with people whose experience and outlook are different to your own.

We hope the structure is self-explanatory, and we hope that the book is written in a way that will be interesting and accessible to the reader. We have included a number of 'exercises' in the text (there is a list of them at the beginning of the book), which could be used in a variety of ways. Readers may simply read through them as part of the text (and you will find that the text refers back to them from time to time), or alternatively they may like to take time out to work on them. The exercises could also be extracted from the text and used as a basis for discussion in seminars and lectures.

PART 1

FOUNDATIONS OF VALUES AND ETHICS

1

WHAT ARE VALUES AND ETHICS?

- What do we mean by 'values'?
- Values as a guide to action
- Values and value systems
- Values and social work
- Personal values
- Societal values
- Values in tension
- What do we mean by 'ethics'?

In the course of your training as a social worker, and in your professional career, you will often hear the phrase 'social work values' and you will also often hear, and engage in, talk about 'professional ethics' and about 'ethical' and 'unethical' practice. Most social workers like to think that, at the core of their practice, there is a particular set of values to do with supporting people in overcoming the pressures and challenges that life and/or an unfair society, has placed upon them. Most social workers would also agree that their job frequently places them in the position of having to make ethical decisions: what, in a moral sense, is the right thing to do. In fact, ethical questions are central to the whole endeavour of social work, as they are to any profession, because social work is an activity that has an impact on the lives of human beings.

The whole book will explore issues to do with values and ethics that you will encounter in your training and in practice. This first chapter will prepare the ground by discussing what we mean by those terms. Before going any further, you might like to put the book down and attempt to write your own definitions. You'll then be able to compare our perspective with your own.

WHAT DO WE MEAN BY 'VALUES'?

> **Value**
>
> 1 '... the regard that something is held to deserve, the importance, worth or usefulness of something: [as in] your support is of great value ...'.
>
> 2 '... principles or standards of behaviour: one's judgement about what is important in life: [as in] they internalize their parents' rules and values ...'. (*Oxford Dictionary of English*, 2009)

The word 'value' is used in a number of ways which, at first sight, do not seem to have a huge amount in common. It is used in a financial way, as in 'gold has a higher value than lead', or in a personal way, as in 'I value your company'. Or we can speak of values in a cultural sense, as in 'Islamic values', 'liberal values' or 'middle-class values'. We also speak of 'value systems'.

Although 'the value of gold' and 'value systems' are very different kinds of idea, there is nevertheless a common ground of meaning. It lies, we suggest, in the notion of preference or choice. When we say to someone 'I value your company', we are really saying that their company is important to us, and that we would choose their company over other things. If an expert on jewellery values your gold ring at £200, he is saying that given the choice between the ring and a sum of money, you should not choose the money unless it is £200 or more.

Similarly, when we speak about the 'value system' of a particular culture, we are referring to the things that culture gives a high priority or importance to when making choices. In a liberal democracy, for instance, a high value is given to personal freedom. ('Everyone has the right to liberty', says the European Convention on Human Rights.) In other societies, personal freedom may be seen as less important than other things, such as the observance of religious rules, or family loyalty, or social cohesion. We cannot really say that one set of values is 'better' than another in any final sense. We can only note that different cultures use different sets of criteria to make choices, presumably as a result of different circumstances and different traditions.

VALUES AS A GUIDE TO ACTION

If all the meanings of the word 'value' relate, as we have suggested, to the idea of choice, then they also relate to ideas about what we *ought* to do. In fact, it would be impossible to make choices *without* values. A purely factual analysis of any given situation can only ever tell us how things are, and what might be the consequences of different courses of action, but this will not, of itself, tell us what we ought to do, unless we have some means of determining which set of consequences is preferable. This principle is sometimes known as Hume's law, after the eighteenth-century philosopher David Hume (see Hume, 2007 [1739]: 335), and is often summarised as 'you can't derive an *ought* from an *is*'.

To give an illustration: imagine you are driving to an important meeting – about, say, the future of a child in care – to which you feel you have an important contribution to make. You are on a motorway driving at over 70 mph, but, due to being held up earlier in the journey, you are in danger of arriving late. Should you increase your speed still further? If you go faster, you are more likely to make your meeting on time and be able to make your contribution, but you are also more likely to have a crash and hurt someone, and of course (in the UK) you would be breaking the law. These are the facts of the matter. Your decision as to what you ought to do will be based on what *value* you place on arriving on time as against the value you place on not endangering yourself and other drivers and/or on sticking to the laws of the land. These are things that the facts in themselves cannot determine for you (though see Chapter 5 for more thoughts on this).

In the social arena, the word 'ought' often carries the implication of some sort of obligation to others, or sometimes to our own future selves (as in 'I really ought to stop smoking'), and it refers to a duty to be fulfilled by either an individual or a group of individuals. The question as to how we arrive at these duties, or 'oughts', is something that we will come back to in the next chapter.

VALUES AND VALUE SYSTEMS

At any given moment of time, we value different things, and this may vary according to our mood or circumstances, but most of us also subscribe to a set of values which is not quite so changeable and which some of us may even be able to define or give a name to: 'I am a Muslim', 'I am a socialist', 'I am a feminist', 'I believe everyone has the right to …', 'I believe a parent ought to …'.

For most of us, beliefs of these kinds are an important cornerstone of our existence, acting as a filter which defines the things we accept or reject, and as a driving force that makes us jump one way as opposed to another. They shape the way we think, the judgements we make, the perceptions we hold about people, and the companions we choose to spend our time with. They are an important part of how we define ourselves: part of who we are. These more enduring and defining sets of values are what are described as *value systems*.

As our examples have already illustrated, a 'value system' is not necessarily an individual matter. When we talk about 'middle-class values', 'British values' or 'Christian values', for instance, we are talking about values that are seen as defining not only an individual but a whole body of people. Many people argue that 'Britishness' or being 'American', for instance, can be partly defined in terms of values, as David Cameron, the British Prime Minister at the time of writing, asserted in a speech in early 2011:

> David Cameron will today signal a sea-change in the government fight against home-grown terrorism, saying the state must confront, and not consort with, the non-violent Muslim groups that are ambiguous about British values such as equality between sexes, democracy and integration.
>
> To belong in Britain is to believe in these values, he will say. (Wintour, 2011: online)

Needless to say, this was a view that was not shared by everyone in Britain. (Is it really possible to say that someone who does not believe in democracy or in the equality of the sexes is somehow not *British* when, not so very long ago, women in Britain were denied the vote, not least by Mr Cameron's own party?) The very contentiousness of the Prime Minister's remarks illustrates an important aspect of value systems. They are usually *contested*. Two British people may both be proud of their British values, and yet disagree profoundly about what British values consist of. Two Muslims may both be strongly committed to Muslim values, yet may still disagree as to what Muslim values are. And this applies to 'social work values' too. We can all agree they are important, but we may still disagree as to what they include.

These are complicated questions, but for the moment, we suggest you might like to give some thought to your own value system, and how it interacts with the value systems of others.

EXERCISE 1.1

THE VALUES BEHIND YOUR CHOICES

The following are examples of different kinds of choice. Think about how you would decide on what choice to make in each case, and ask yourself what set of values you would base your choice on:

- Your daughter is exceptionally able academically. A wealthy relative offers to pay for her to attend a prestigious private school, where she will be able to have much more individual attention from teachers and a programme much more tailored to her individual needs than she would at your local comprehensive. Do you accept the offer?
- In a supermarket you have a choice between buying two packets of tea of similar quality: one is more expensive because the company that produces it pays a good price to the

growers; the other is cheaper because the company that produces it pays the absolute minimum to the growers.

- You are married. Your partner's best friend tells you that they find you very attractive and suggests an affair. Do you tell your partner about this incident?
- You are a social worker. You are visiting a single parent who is struggling emotionally and financially. She tells you that she is supplementing her income by dealing in crack cocaine, and asks for your assurance that you will tell no one about it. Crack cocaine is a major problem in the area where she lives. What do you say?

Comments on Exercise 1.1

The choice you make will probably be based in part on your estimation of the likely outcomes of the various choices available to you. (Do you think your daughter would enjoy being in a private school and do well there?) But it will also be based on what value system you subscribe to. (Do you believe in private education? Do you think openness is always the most important thing in relationships, or is it sometimes better to keep things to yourself?) Often these kinds of decisions are difficult because they entail balancing competing, and perhaps contradictory, values. ('I think my daughter would be happier in the private school and I believe I ought to do my very best for my daughter, but I also disapprove of private schooling'; 'I want to be truthful with my partner, but I don't want to wreck a friendship'.)

In the last example, however – where your client admits to dealing in drugs – the decision to be made is not simply a personal one. Your agency would have its own expectations and perhaps written guidelines about how to deal with such a situation (for example, guidelines about confidentiality and its limits).

VALUES AND SOCIAL WORK

The final example in Exercise 1.1 illustrates that when we move from our private life to our professional life, the concept of 'values' takes on an additional dimension. Value questions don't go away when we put on our professional 'hat' – far from it – but they cease to be purely personal. As Kerstin Svensson observes:

> Outside the organization, 'doing good' is just a personal matter ... Within the organization, social work does not just entail 'doing good' but also includes the exercise of power and influence ... It is thus necessary to understand the concept of 'doing good' from a perspective where the organizational aspects are taken into consideration. (Svensson, 2009: 235)

In other words, when you are a paid professional, you cannot just pretend that your relationships with your clients are of the same kind as your relationships with people you know in your private life, for you carry the powers and responsibilities conferred on you by your job. All professions therefore have ethical codes which aim, among other things, to prevent the abuse and misuse of power, but social workers in particular, because they typically work with the least powerful people in society, need to be aware of the exercise of power and control that they are actually engaged in on a daily basis.

In social work, because of its socially determined nature and its focus on human interactions, you will be constantly involved in judgements in which competing values have to be weighed up. At a number of different levels, social workers are provided with frameworks, sometimes contradictory and sometimes contentious, within which to make these decisions.

THE LEVEL OF LEGISLATION

Various principles are enshrined in the framework of laws, policies, government guidelines and agency rules within which social work operates. These principles are based, implicitly or explicitly, on certain values, as Exercise 1.2 illustrates.

EXERCISE 1.2

VALUES IMPLICIT IN LAWS

In English and Welsh law, the 1983 Mental Health Act, Section 3, states that an Approved Social Worker (or an Approved Mental Health Professional, following the changes made by the 2007 Mental Health Act) can make an application for a person to be admitted to hospital and detained there for treatment, only if certain conditions are met, including that:

- he is suffering from mental illness, severe mental impairment, psychopathic disorder or mental impairment and his mental disorder is of a nature or degree which makes it appropriate for him to receive medical treatment in a hospital; and
- in the case of psychopathic disorder or mental impairment, such treatment is likely to alleviate or prevent a deterioration of his condition; and
- it is necessary for the health and safety of the patient or the protection of other persons that he should receive such treatment and it cannot be provided unless he is detained under this section.

What values are implied by this? What alternative viewpoints might there be?

Comments on Exercise 1.2

The law says that a person cannot be detained simply because they are mentally ill, but only if their own health or safety is at risk, or if they are endangering others. It therefore tries to strike a balance between protecting individual liberty and protecting the welfare of mentally ill people and the public. So there are competing values embedded here, with the law attempting to strike a balance between:

- the right to personal liberty;
- the right of the general public to protection; and
- the right, in some circumstances, to be protected against ourselves.

Because it is a compromise, this means that some people who are mentally ill, and are unhappy as a result, cannot be made to accept medical help, even if that help would make them feel better. Those who drafted the legislation obviously felt that this was a price worth paying in order to protect liberty. This is a value judgement. You may take the view that it should be made easier to compulsorily treat people who are not able to make a rational judgement themselves about their best interests.

On the other hand, you might think the legislation makes it too easy to detain people. After all, the normal principle is that a person cannot be detained unless they can be proved to have done something wrong. It would not normally be regarded as acceptable to deprive someone of their liberty just because it was thought they were likely to do something wrong in the future. So why should it be possible to detain a person who happens to be (in the opinion of doctors) 'mentally disordered', even if they haven't as yet harmed anyone?

The position you take really depends on the relative value you place on welfare and liberty.

The principles enshrined in legislation are not necessarily in harmony with one another. They can and do conflict. Nor are they necessarily in harmony with other aspects of government decision making. For instance, the legislation may enshrine one principle, but government policy, at the local or national level, may make that principle impossible to achieve in practice (for example, if there is insufficient funding). The principles enshrined in legislation may also conflict with professional ethics. Donald Dixon (2009: 266), writing in particular about the child protection field, notes that 'ethical and legal standards are not always co-terminous'. He points out that there are ways of behaving that are not illegal, but still not ethical according to normal professional standards (for example, it is not actually illegal to be rude and overbearing with service users), and there are ways of behaving that may be illegal, but which social workers may feel to be their ethical obligation.

THE LEVEL OF POLICY AND PROCEDURE

In addition to the framework provided by the law, government provides guidelines and procedures which agencies are required to follow, and individual agencies have their own documents ranging from broad 'mission statements' to detailed procedural manuals. Sometimes these documents include explicit statements about an organisation's values, and about the ethical principles it attempts to follow. This is particularly the case with mission statements, such as the following from the British children's charity, Barnado's:

> Barnardo's believes in children regardless of their circumstances, gender, race, disability or behaviour.
>
> We believe in the abused, the vulnerable, the forgotten and the neglected. We will support them, stand up for them and bring out the best in each and every child.
>
> We do this because we believe that every child deserves the best start in life and the chance to fulfil their potential.
>
> We use the knowledge gained from our direct work with children to campaign for better childcare policy and to champion the rights of every child.
>
> With the right help, committed support and a little belief, even the most vulnerable children can turn their lives around. Barnardo's is regulated by the Charity Commission. Being a registered charity means that we must always be accountable and transparent. (Barnado's, 2011: online)

Often, guidelines and policy documents do not make explicit statements of values. Nevertheless, it is always possible to discern the value assumptions that lie behind such documents, just as it is possible to identify the values underlying laws, as we showed in Exercise 1.2.

THE LEVEL OF AGENCY PRIORITIES

If someone said 'I really value your opinion' but then never let you get a word in without immediately interrupting or contradicting you, you might well question whether they really *did* respect your opinion so very much. What people say and what they do are not necessarily the same. Whether looking at yourself, or some other person, or an organisation – or indeed a whole society – it is necessary to look behind words and stated intentions to get an idea of the values that really guide actions.

   If you want to understand an agency's values therefore, it is important to look at its priorities *in practice* as well as its stated intentions. Consider, for instance, an agency that stated that it was committed to working *preventatively* or *proactively*. If you looked at the way it responded to new referrals and found out that they were only ever followed up if they were dire emergencies, you would have to conclude that, in fact, working preventatively was not a priority for that agency, whatever it might say, or whatever its staff might like to think. Words and deeds are not necessarily the same thing, but it is not uncommon in social work for virtuous-sounding words ('partnership', 'empowerment', 'person-centred') to be used rather freely, as if words themselves were equivalent to actual behaviour. (For more on 'virtuous words', see Beckett, 2009. We will come back to this in Chapter 5.)

   So, part of the values framework within which a social worker operates is their agency's *priorities* and its expectations *in practice* about the ways things should be dealt with, which may or may not be reflected in the agency's public statements about its values.

THE LEVEL OF PROFESSIONAL ETHICS AND PROFESSIONAL VALUES

Another way in which values are, so to speak, enshrined are in guidelines on professional ethics, drawn up to try and establish certain standards of conduct. Doctors, lawyers and accountants all have their codes of professional ethics, as do social workers. Underlying these formal codes typically are certain values which are seen as being core to that profession.

These ethical guidelines, and the professional values that lie behind them, set a different kind of framework of expectations around professionals which is distinct from those created by legislation, policies and agency priorities. The job of a doctor is different in different settings – a heart surgeon and a GP have very different tasks to perform – and yet certain ethical principles, and a certain professional ethos, are supposed to be common to all doctors. The same is true of social work. And it can happen that professional values come into conflict with the values inherent in legislation or policy or agency guidelines.

PERSONAL VALUES

A professional social worker – or indeed any other professional – cannot only be guided by her personal values, but she cannot simply disregard her own personal values either. Personal values, after all, lie behind the decision to go into social work rather than into some other occupation. Many people who go into social work are motivated by a belief that it is important to do something for those who are excluded or disadvantaged by society at large. Some are motivated by religious beliefs or political convictions. Your own personal values will also inevitably influence how you do your job and the decisions and choices that you make. For this reason, it is important to be as aware as possible of what those values are and where they come from. You may like to use the following exercise to reflect on your own values before reading further.

YOUR PERSONAL VALUES

List some of the basic beliefs you have about what is 'right' and what you think is 'wrong', particularly those beliefs you feel most strongly about. What would your friends identify as things that you feel strongly about?

- Examine these beliefs and ask yourself which ones you would regard as the most central and enduring. Which would you most readily describe as being 'part of who you are'?
- Identify some of the influences upon your life that have helped shape those beliefs. Would you identify any of them as being part of a 'value system'? If you are Jewish, for instance,

EXERCISE 1.3

(Cont'd)

you might identify some of your beliefs as having been instilled in you by Jewish culture. Or you might subscribe to a set of beliefs which you describe as 'socialist' or 'feminist'. Even things like what newspaper you prefer to read might to some extent loosely define a value system to which you subscribe.

- Consider how your beliefs/values might have shaped you differently if you were brought up in a different country, or at a different time in history.
- Consider how your beliefs/values might be different if you had been brought up in a different family or a different social class.
- To what extent do you think your gender makes a difference to the way you view the world and the values you consider to be important?

Comments on Exercise 1.3

We don't know, of course, what you may have come up with in this exercise. We can only say that the two authors of this book subscribe in many respects to very different value systems, which can be seen as in part the product of personal choice and in part the product of very different backgrounds. One of us is black, one is white. One of us has a strong commitment to a particular religion (Christianity), the other does not subscribe to a religion. One of us comes from a family that has been rooted in Britain for many generations, while the other has family roots in the Caribbean. As a result of these sorts of differences, we bring different priorities and assumptions to our work. (And yet, at the same time, in spite of these differences, we also find that we have a good deal in common and were able to collaborate on this book.)

Having looked at your values in general terms, we would now like to move on directly to look at the way in which you might apply your values to a decision of a kind that you might have to make in a social work context.

EXERCISE 1.4

VALUES AND CHOICES

Resources are necessarily finite and social workers are often involved, in all kinds of ways, in decisions about who gets a service and who does not.

Imagine that you work for an agency which provides some financial help for single parents under pressure who would like daycare for their children. You are part of a panel which decides on the allocation of funds. There is just enough money in the budget to provide assistance to one family, and you have four applicants. On what basis should you make your recommendation? And why?

(a) The parent and child you like the best.
(b) The parent or child who reminds you of your own personal circumstances.

(c) The parent who you think is most intimidating and likely to be 'difficult' if not given the place.
(d) The parent and child whose circumstances you find the most touching.
(e) The parent you regard as most deserving of help.
(f) The ethnic background of the parent or child.
(g) The gender of the parent.
(h) The needs of the child.
(i) The needs of the parent.
(j) The needs of the playgroup.

Comments on Exercise 1.4

You will probably agree that (a)–(d) are not an appropriate basis on which to make such a decision. But if you have ever been in a situation of this kind, you will know that it can be very difficult to eliminate such factors from one's thoughts, particularly in border-line situations. As to why it is wrong to make decisions on such a basis, we suggest that it is because to do so is quite literally unprofessional: we are being paid to perform a specific role for society, not to indulge our private preferences.

What about the question of which applicant is the most 'deserving'? This seems to us to be a moral judgement about which of the applicants is the 'better' person – and does not fit with a professional role. Who are we to judge in this way? In the nineteenth century, however, welfare agencies did make a very sharp distinction between the deserving and the undeserving poor.

You almost certainly said that ethnic background is not an appropriate basis for such decision making. This is not to say, however, that specific services should never be targeted at specific ethnic groups. African-Caribbean children in the looked-after system, for instance, may require specific help in connection with hair and skin care which is different from the help required by white children. But this is a question of different needs, not of giving preferential treatment to one group over another.

When it comes to gender, single fathers are much rarer than single mothers and some-times, in our experience, are given preferential treatment by professional services. You may like to consider this and ask yourself whether – and, if so, on what basis – it might be justified. It seems to us that, as in the case of ethnicity, it can be justified only if it can be demonstrated that single fathers have different needs from single mothers. (Perhaps they are more socially isolated and have less peer-group support, for instance?)

You may well have thought that both the needs of the parent and of the child were appropriate bases for decision making. In fact, under the 1989 Children Act, it is ultimately the need of the child not the parent that is supposed to be the determining factor, but in practice the needs of parent and child often coincide, or are interconnected at least.

(Cont'd)

The needs of the playgroup itself must also be relevant, since if the playgroup's needs are not taken into account it would in the long run be all the group's users who lost out. Thus, even if she is clearly identified to be most in need, it may not be appropriate to recommend a child to the playgroup who is known to present difficult and disruptive behaviour, if this is likely to jeopardise the functioning of the group as a whole.

The point that this exercise is intended to illustrate is that there are certain kinds of value judgement that we as individuals inevitably make (such as whether or not we like a person) which should have no place in our practice as professionals. The appropriate basis for the kinds of decision illustrated by the exercise should be an assessment of needs. But we should be under no illusions that by focusing on needs we have somehow avoided the problem of value judgements. Weighing up one person's needs against another is a matter of judgement and cannot be done without making decisions about what kinds of needs are more or less important than others. In most situations, there are also questions of competing and perhaps conflicting needs – the needs of the parent, the child and the playgroup in the above example – which have to be weighed up one against another.

Your judgements on these matters are inevitably going to be influenced by your own beliefs and your own life experience. If you have personal experience of poverty or of lone parenthood or of domestic violence, for instance, you may take a different view of cases where poverty or lone parenthood are factors than a social worker without personal experience of these things. If you have strong views that small children should, as far as possible, be cared for by their parents and not left with professional carers, then you may take a different position from a person who believes very strongly that lone parents should, as of right, be given the necessary support with childcare to allow them to pursue a career.

It is impossible to eliminate these personal values from professional decision making. It is possible, though, to keep our values and assumptions under review, and be open to other arguments and ideas. It is also possible to recognise that certain preferences or beliefs are irrelevant to the task in hand and should be disregarded.

SOCIETAL VALUES

Some years ago, when working as a social worker, one of us was going to visit a client, got lost, and stopped to ask the way from a boy in the street. The boy looked him up and down. 'Social worker, are you?' he asked. Social workers may not wear a uniform but the boy was able to make an accurate guess all the same, on the basis of dress and demeanour. However much we might like to see ourselves as doing things our own way, the fact is that most of us tend to fit into a pattern, and this is true of our values and beliefs as well as of our dress sense.

Although we are all unique, the values we hold are much less individual than we would perhaps like to think. They are shaped in large part by the society around us and by the particular subsection of society in which we find ourselves: our age group, our gender, our ethnic community, our geographical community, our occupational group, our class, and so on.

We do not notice this all the time because we tend to assume that the values we share with those around us are just 'common sense'. It is really only when we compare the kinds of assumptions we make now with those made at other times, or that are made now in other places or in other sections of society, that we realise that many of the values that we take for granted are not inevitable, but are the result of a particular and local consensus. The following is a random selection of examples of ways in which societal values can be seen to have changed over time:

- *Sexual behaviour*. In Britain, there has been a huge shift in the last 50 years in what is regarded as acceptable sexual behaviour. Premarital sex is accepted as the norm. Homosexual relationships have shifted from being prohibited by law to being a form of relationship that can be formalised by law though civil partnerships. (This is of course not a shift that has occurred in all societies – yet – and there are still countries in the world where homosexuality is punishable by death, and where premarital sex can lead to social disgrace.)
- *Corporal punishment*. Fifty years ago, caning and other forms of corporal punishment were seen as normal and acceptable in schools and at home. Birching was a sentence available to the courts. Now, in several countries, even smacking with the hand is illegal, although there are still countries where flogging is a normal punishment under the law.
- *Attitudes to childhood*. Historically, and in more traditional societies today, an emphasis is placed on the duties and obligations of children towards their parents. 'Honour thy father and mother', for instance, is one of the Ten Commandments in the Old Testament. In contemporary Britain, the obligations and duties are seen mainly as flowing in the other direction, as is evidenced by the principle enshrined in Section 1 of the 1989 Children Act that 'the child's welfare should be the paramount consideration'.
- *Freedom of expression*. Almost half a century ago, D.H. Lawrence's novel, *Lady Chatterley's Lover*, was the subject of an obscenity trial. Nowadays, whether we like it or not, explicit pornography is freely available in convenience stores all over Britain and other Western countries.
- *Supervision of children*. Forty years ago, it was normal for quite young children to be allowed to spend long periods away from their homes without parental supervision, playing with friends. Perhaps due to increasing media coverage of incidents where children have been killed or abducted, children are far more restricted now. Parental behaviour that once would have been regarded as normal, and even healthy, would now be regarded as neglectful and irresponsible.
- *The sanctity of life*. Although the idea of human life as something sacred and precious is a very persistent value, the consensual view has certainly changed in respect of the circumstances under which the taking of life is justified, and remains markedly different in different cultures. The death penalty, for instance, was historically used in Britain as a punishment, not only for murder but even for lesser crimes, but (although it is still used in many parts of the world, including many US states) it is no longer used anywhere in the European Union. By contrast, though abortion and euthanasia are still regarded by many people as unacceptable ways of taking human lives, both are much more openly discussed than in the past and abortion is legal – and even provided by the state – in Britain.

You will be able to think of many other examples of areas in which the accepted wisdom of society at large about what is 'right' or 'appropriate' or 'normal' has radically changed in very recent times, and examples too of radical differences in attitude between contemporary societies and cultures: ideas about the roles of men and women, for instance, or attitudes to old people or people who are mentally ill.

Societal values are instilled in us by a socialisation process that begins, for most of us, with the messages we receive from our parents about what is important in life, but is then built upon by many other influences: schooling, the peer group and, very importantly in modern culture, the mass media, which constantly, both explicitly and implicitly, offer us sets of values to absorb.

But even though our personal values may be shaped in large part by the values of the society around us – or the values of the part of society to which we belong – this does not mean that there is no room for conflict. It is inevitable, not only in personal contexts but in professional ones, that we will find ourselves disagreeing with other people about value questions. And it is equally inevitable that even widely held values, with which few people would disagree, will frequently come into conflict *with one another*. In Exercise 1.2, we looked at the 1983 Mental Health Act in England and Wales, and noted that it attempts to balance important yet fundamentally contradictory principles: (a) the state should respect individual liberty; (b) the state should protect the public and vulnerable people.

It is in the nature of social work that it is prone to finding itself in difficult places where deeply held societal values collide. Because this involves making compromises in which one principle is partly sacrificed for another, this can often result in social workers seeming, in the eyes of others, to trample on one or other of those deeply held values. For instance, on the one hand, because it is a strongly and widely held belief that family life is sacrosanct and private, social workers intervening in families can easily be seen as interfering and oppressive, transgressing against a deep taboo. On the other hand, since it is also a strongly and widely held belief that childhood is precious and that children should be protected from harm, the failure of social workers to intervene in families to protect children may be greeted with horror and *also* be seen as transgressive.

Because these societal values exist not only outside of us but also inside, social workers need to be prepared not only for the condemnation of others, but also for powerful feelings of guilt, even if they are clear in their own minds that they have taken the best possible course of action in the circumstances. The example in Exercise 1.5 illustrates this.

EXERCISE 1.5

TAKING GERALDINE'S BABY

Geraldine, aged 23, was a victim in childhood of sexual and physical abuse, emotional rejection and neglect. She is a vulnerable person who has very low self-esteem, has made several suicide attempts and is very easily led. As an adult, she has a history of entering into relationships with violent, abusive men. She is a heroin user. She has just given birth to her third child, a baby boy.

Her two previous babies have been adopted. The first baby, whom she had at the age of 16, was taken into care when Geraldine disappeared for two weeks, leaving the baby in the care of a 13-year-old girl to whom she gave £5 to look after him. The second was brain-damaged as a result of shaking by Geraldine's then partner. This occurred when Geraldine had moved in with him in secret, while pretending to live at another address. This had been against a specific undertaking that she made to the professional agencies to allow no contact between him and the baby in view of his known history of violence to other children.

The new baby is likely to present particular management problems due to Geraldine's heroin use during pregnancy. (The effect of withdrawal from heroin on a newborn baby is known as Neonatal Abstinence Syndrome and can produce a range of effects, including irritability, sleeping and feeding problems, prolonged screaming, fever, vomiting and diarrhoea.)

Geraldine's current boyfriend, who is not the father of the baby, is another man with a history of violence against Geraldine and others.

A decision has been reached by a pre-birth child protection conference that Geraldine's baby should be removed from her immediately at birth. Because of Geraldine's history of hiding from the authorities and running away, the conference exceptionally decided that Geraldine should not be informed of this decision in advance.

As a social worker, you and a police officer are to attend the hospital to arrange for the removal of the new baby to a foster home under a police protection order. When you arrive, Geraldine is nursing the baby, looking radiantly happy. She knows you, and when she sees you she smiles and tells you that this time she knows she is going to get it right and give this little boy all the love she herself never received.

How would you react?

Comments on Exercise 1.5

However necessary it was for the baby's safety for him to be taken from his mother, there can be few people who would not feel very badly about removing a child from a mother under such circumstances. There is surely no society in which the bond between mother and baby is not seen as something precious. And in any case, it feels wrong to shatter the happiness of a young woman who has experienced so little happiness in her life.

In such situations, one may be tempted to back-track on the agreed plan in some way, or to dilute the painful message that needs to be given.

Nevertheless, if a decision has been reached, after proper consideration of the possible consequences of all the available courses of action, then it would be wrong to allow your own feelings to deflect you from carrying out that course of action – and in fact you are not at liberty to do so, since the plan is not your individual one but one that has been agreed between all the agencies.

None of these arguments, however, is likely to change the way that you and the police officer will feel about carrying out the case conference decision.

VALUES IN TENSION

Social workers are called upon to perform many complex tasks that involve difficult human interactions and in some instances involve overruling what would
normally be regarded as an individual's rights (for instance: compulsory detention
under mental health legislation, separation of children and parents under childcare
legislation or the enforcement of court orders on young offenders under youth
justice legislation). In trying to come to the right decision about how to respond in
any given situation, the social worker struggles not only with her own personal
feelings, the limitations of her own skill and knowledge, and the constraints
imposed by the real world of limited options, she also struggles with a plethora of
competing values – societal values, personal values, professional values and the
prevailing values of her agency (see Figure 1.1).

This struggle may be experienced as conflict *within* the individual between different and competing personal values and/or internalised societal values (as we
tried to illustrate in Exercise 1.5) but the struggle may also take the form of
disagreements with others. It may involve disagreement with colleagues about
how to proceed. (Your strongly held view might be that 'Mrs Brown may be a

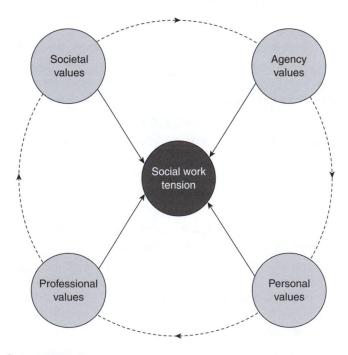

Figure 1.1 Competing values

little confused but we should still respect her right to take risks if she wants to do so'. Your colleague's strongly held view might be that 'We owe it to Mrs Brown to take steps to protect her against the consequences of her own impaired judgement'.) It may entail disagreements with service users. (Your position – and your agency's position – may be that 'beating your children is unacceptable'. A parent's position may be: 'You have no right to tell me how to bring up my children. I was always beaten and it never did me any harm at all'.) It may involve struggles with managers or other agencies. There are endless arenas, internal and external, within which value conflicts are played out. Figure 1.2 attempts to illustrate these wider complexities.

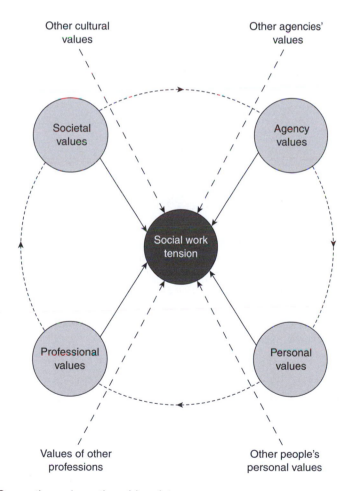

Figure 1.2 Competing values: the wider picture

WHAT DO WE MEAN BY 'ETHICS'?

Although we have explored the word 'values', we have not yet attempted a defini-tion of 'ethics'. It is a word with several meanings, but all of them rather narrower and more specific than that of 'values'. Ethics relate not just to our overall stance on life, or to our general notions of what is important, but to actual rules, codes or principles of conduct. Since these rules and principles will always ultimately be based on a values system of some kind, ethics can be seen as the practical applica-tion of values. 'Human life is sacred', for example, is a pretty universal value, from which flows the ethical principle that it is wrong, at least in most circumstances, to kill. Likewise, 'privacy is important' is a value which forms the basis of professional obligations to respect the confidentiality of clients. Dubois and Miley (2008: 111) suggest that 'whereas values are the implicit or explicit beliefs about what people consider good, ethics relates to what people consider correct or right'.

In social work, a distinction can also be made between, on the one hand, profes-sional ethics – the principles of conduct, enshrined in various codes, which are broadly similar to those followed by other professions – and, on the other hand, the 'emanci-patory values', broader and more political in character, which are particularly char-acteristic of social work. This reflects the fact that while other professions (teachers, doctors, lawyers) work with people from across the whole of society, social workers' particular focus is on the least powerful groups in society.

CHAPTER SUMMARY

This chapter has been an exploration of what we mean by 'values' and 'ethics'. We have considered the meaning of the words themselves, arguing that 'values' are an indis-pensable (indeed unavoidable) component of decision making in a personal or profes-sional context. We have looked at different kinds of values, including the values that are contained, implicitly or explicitly, in laws, policies and agency practice, as well as societal and personal values. We have considered the tensions and contradictions that can arise between competing values, and we have offered a view of 'ethics' as rules of principles of behaviour that flow from values.

A more specialist use of the word 'ethics' is a name given to the branch of philosophy, also called 'moral philosophy', that considers the nature of morality. This is the topic we explore in the next chapter.

 FURTHER READING

We hope that this book will offer a balanced introduction to the subject of values and ethics in social work, but of course every book necessarily reflects the views (and indeed the values) of its authors. We therefore recommend that you read more widely and also look at other introductions to the subject. These include the following books by Sarah Banks (whose fourth edition appeared soon after we had completed this manuscript) and by Lester Parrott:

Banks, S. (2012) *Ethics and Values in Social Work*, 4th edn. Basingtoke: Palgrave.

Parrott, L. (2010) *Values and Ethics in Social Work Practice,* 2nd edn. Exeter: Learning Matters.

2

MORAL PHILOSOPHY

- Thinking about right and wrong
- Duties and rights
- Consequences
- Virtues
- Structure and power

We all believe that some actions are right and some are wrong, but what is the basis on which we make that judgement? The question is more complicated than it seems at first glance, for we don't all agree on what is right and wrong, and ideas about what is right and wrong change over time and vary from one culture to another. (To give an example we used in the previous chapter, in the UK in the past, and in many cultures today, sex before marriage would have been seen as seriously morally wrong, though we would guess that only a fairly small minority in the UK would now see this as a major moral issue and many, if not most, would not see it as a moral issue at all.)

But if there are so many different views about what is right and what is wrong, who is to say which view is the correct one, and how are we to work out the right thing to do if we are not sure? There are no simple answers to these questions, but philosophers, over many thousands of years, have tried to clarify the different ways in which we might come to such decisions. In this chapter, we will look at some of the main approaches under the following headings:

- *Duties and rights*. This is the idea that, just by being human, we are entitled to expect certain treatment from others, and required to treat other human beings likewise. Under this heading, we will discuss in particular the influence of the philosopher Immanuel Kant.
- *Consequences*. This is the idea that the rightness or wrongness of an action should be judged by weighing up its positive and negative consequences. Under this heading, we will discuss the utilitarian philosophers.

- *Virtues.* This is the idea that the rightness or wrongness of an action is not so much about duties, rights or consequences, as about what kind of behaviour is likely to make us grow and thrive as human beings, an approach dating back to the Greek philosopher Aristotle. Under this general heading, we will also discuss the feminist 'ethics of care'.
- *Structure and power.* This is the idea that the rightness and wrongness of actions cannot be divorced from politics, so that the vital question becomes 'Whose interest would this serve?'

THINKING ABOUT RIGHT AND WRONG

We do not want to give the impression that these ideas are the personal possessions of philosophers alone, for philosophers look at the kinds of questions that every thinking person asks themselves from time to time. ('How did we get here?', 'What is life's purpose?', 'How do we know what's real and what isn't?' These are philosophical questions, but they are also questions that regularly occur to small children.) People with no philosophical training at all, when talking about issues of right and wrong, use all the different approaches we discuss in this chapter, even if they have never heard of any of the philosophers we name.

What is more, in spite of the obvious and substantial differences between people and between cultures, human beings do tend to broadly agree about what is right and wrong. As James Rachels (1999: 27–9) observes, all societies agree that it is wrong to lie, that it is important to care for children, and that killing people is wrong (albeit, in the latter case, with various exceptions that we will discuss shortly). Rachels argues that the differences between cultures may represent adaptation to different circumstances, rather than fundamentally different underlying values, and, if you agree with him, you might be tempted to conclude that the difference between right and wrong is just obvious, just something that everybody knows.

But social work will confront you with exceptionally difficult ethical questions: 'When is it morally justified to remove a child from a parent?', 'When is it appropriate to override the wishes of a service user?', 'Who should we give a service to when we can't give a service to everyone who needs it?' This means that it is worth thinking with some care about the basis on which you base your ethical judgements, and for this reason it is useful to tease out the 'competing accounts of morality' (Deigh, 2010: 196) that philosophers describe, to allow you to weigh up their pros and cons.

Later in the chapter, in order to illustrate the different approaches we will use an imaginary scenario in which a decision is to be made about how to respond to financial cuts in children's social care (writing in 2011, this seemed to us to be particularly relevant, but the allocation of limited resources is always an ethical challenge). For the moment, here is a much more general question: *Why is it wrong to kill people?*

In every society, now and in the past, it has been generally accepted that it is wrong to kill people, even though most, if not all, societies have attached various caveats and exceptions. In the present day, some of these exceptions include killing in war, the death penalty (in countries ranging from Saudi Arabia to the USA), euthanasia and abortion. In the past, they have included such circumstances as gladiatorial contests (in the Roman Empire), sacrifices to the gods (for example in the Aztec civilisation of Mexico) and infanticide (the killing of newborn babies, which might occur when the community did not have the resources to provide for them).

Some cultures and individuals apply the idea that it is wrong to kill not only human beings but also other species. Strict adherents of the Jain religion, for example, are not just vegetarian but even try to avoid accidentally stepping on insects. However, this is exceptional and we would guess that there is a majority view across the world that it is wrong to kill people, but that the same rules do not apply to animals. Indeed, many people think it is acceptable to kill animals not only for food but for the advancement of science, for fashion or even for entertainment (bullfighting, fox hunting, angling).

Readers of this book will have different views as to the limits and permissible exceptions to the general principle that it is wrong to kill. Some will be vegetarians or vegans; others will enjoy fishing or shooting as sports. Some will be pacifists, while others will regard killing as legitimate in pursuit of just war aims, or as part of a liberation struggle against an oppressive regime. There will be different views on abortion (up to what stage of pregnancy and in what circumstances?), on euthanasia and the death penalty and on sacrificing animals to research. (Is it acceptable to kill animals for cancer research? How about for testing cosmetics? Or in academic research on brain development? Or to test surgical procedures? Or to learn the effects of new weapons systems?)

These differences of view are interesting and important. Nevertheless, it is probably safe to make the assumption that any reader of this book will agree that, at least under most circumstances, *killing people is wrong*.

The question is – why?

EXERCISE 2.1

WHY IS IT WRONG TO KILL?

Exactly why do you regard killing people as wrong? What does 'wrong' mean in this context? In answering these questions, try to question your own assumptions and define the terms you use. For example, if you were to answer 'Killing people is wrong because no one has the right to end another person's life', then you might want to ask what you mean by 'rights' and where you think they come from.

Comments on Exercise 2.1

Here are some of the possible ways in which you might have answered:

1 It is forbidden by God (for example, in the Bible or the Q'uran). If this is your view, you might like to rephrase the above question and ask yourself *why* God forbids

killing. We will not be discussing religion any further in this chapter, but will return to it in the next one.

2 It just is *wrong*. You can't give a reason for it. It's just something you know inside. You might have some support here from the eighteenth-century philosopher David Hume who was sceptical about the possibility of deriving ethical principles by pure reason, and wrote: 'Morality … is more properly felt than judg'd of' (2007 [1739]: 335). The difficulty of relying entirely on this type of argument, though, is that it has no answer to someone who says, 'Well, I don't feel the same way'. If it is really all about feelings, then what makes one feeling any more right than another, and how do we resolve disagreements between ourselves?

3 It's wrong because human life has intrinsic value: a human being isn't just an object that can be disposed of. Here, you are entering the territory of Immanuel Kant and the 'categorical imperative', which we will discuss shortly.

4 It's wrong because a society in which it would be acceptable to kill people would be miserable and dangerous for everybody. This is a more utilitarian argument, based on consequences, which we'll be discussing again shortly.

5 It's wrong because gentleness and tolerance towards others are important qualities which every human being needs to possess in order to thrive. We suspect this is unlikely to be your main argument against killing people, but this *type* of argument is characteristic of virtue ethics, which we will also come back to later.

DUTIES AND RIGHTS

One line of argument that people often use when debating moral questions is to refer to duties or rights. Duties and rights are not the same thing, of course – a person who worries all the time about their rights is coming from a very different place from a person who worries all the time about their duties – but they are opposite sides of the same coin. If you have a right, then it follows that other people have a duty to meet it. If you have a duty, then it follows that other people have a right to expect you to perform it.

But if we accept that human beings have certain unavoidable duties towards other people, and therefore certain rights which they are entitled to expect to be met no matter what, where do these rights and duties come from? The famous text of the American Declaration of Independence, written by Thomas Jefferson, declared that 'We hold these Truths to be self-evident, that all Men are created equal, that they are endowed by their Creator with certain unalienable Rights, that among these are Life, Liberty and the Pursuit of Happiness' (Jefferson, 1776). But why are these truths self-evident? (One might also ask, if they were so self-evident, did Jefferson not think they applied to his own black slaves?) The 1950 European Convention on Human Rights (enshrined in UK law as the 1998 Human Rights Act) declares, among many other things, that 'No one shall be subjected to torture or to inhuman or degrading treatment or punishment', thereby placing a duty on signatories to uphold these rights. But where do these rights and duties come from?

The philosopher Immanuel Kant (1724–1804) is particularly associated with an approach to ethics based on duties, an approach which is sometimes called 'deontological', from the Greek word for duty: *deon*. Kant's position, very roughly described, is that at the root of all duties lies a basic imperative (that is: an unavoidable requirement) that is grounded in the nature of human existence itself. He expressed this categorical imperative in several different ways, including the following:

- Act only on that maxim whereby you can at the same time will that it become a universal law.
- So act as to treat humanity, whether in your own person or in that of any other, never solely as a means but always also as an end. (cited by Norman, 1998: 76)

Although these two statements look, at first sight, very different, at the root of them both lies the idea that it is not reasonable for one person to treat himself or herself as a special case. 'Do as you would be done by', people sometimes say (even if they have never heard of Kant), which is pretty much what the first version of the categorical imperative boils down to, and what they mean by it is that we shouldn't treat others as if they were different to ourselves. If we treat people as means rather than ends (as described in the second version of the imperative), then of course we are making that very mistake, for we are acting as if they were merely objects to be used for our benefit, when (as a matter of fact, and not just of opinion) they are subjects in their own right no less than we are. It can be argued that all other duties and rights – the right not to be tortured, the duty not to kill – flow from this basic starting point: I am human and so are you, and if my thoughts and feelings matter, then so do yours.

Social workers often deal with people who tend to get objectified by the rest of society. Offenders, rough sleepers, drug addicts, asylum seekers and people with mental health problems are all often talked about as if they were problems or nuisances, or threats to the rest of society, rather than human beings and fellow citizens with needs and feelings in their own right. When this occurs, a social work duty that flows directly from Kant's categorical imperative is to show them the respect that is due to them as persons in their own right ('respect for persons'), and to support them in demanding that respect from others, along with the basic rights that flow from it. In practice, though, it is all too easy for beleaguered social workers themselves to end up seeing their clients as problems or threats, and, as one of us has observed elsewhere (Beckett, 2003), this is sometimes reflected in the very language that social workers use. We need to be clear that, if we stop respecting our service users as people, as subjects rather than objects, then we are not only going against the entire ethical basis for our profession, but against what is, according to Kant, the basis of morality itself.

CONSEQUENCES

One way of deciding the right thing to do, used frequently in everyday life, is to look at the consequences of actions (an approach which, for obvious reasons, is referred to as 'consequentialist'). Shortly before this chapter was written (in early 2011), the international community had been debating whether or not it was right for the armed forces of other countries to intervene in support of the uprising in Libya against the dictator Colonel Gaddafi. There were some people who talked about this in terms of duties and rights (there were those, for instance, who argued that to intervene in another country is simply wrong under any circumstances) but most participants in the debate seemed to discuss the question in terms of *consequences*. Would intervening save lives? Would it undermine the legitimacy of the revolution? Would it increase or reduce anti-Western feeling in the Muslim world? Would it set a dangerous precedent? Readers of this book will know more about the outcome of the military action than we knew at the time of writing, and will therefore know the answers to some of these questions, but our point here is that the debate was generally more concerned with likely consequences than with general principles. It took place in largely consequentialist terms.

The most well known consequentialist approach is that of utilitarianism, first fully formulated by Jeremy Bentham (1748–1832) and then further elaborated by his student John Stuart Mill (1806–73). The name comes from the word 'utility' which of course means 'usefulness', and the idea of utilitarianism is that whether an action is right or wrong depends on whether it does more good overall than harm (the greatest good to the greatest number). This may not seem particularly revolutionary today, and may just sound like common sense. 'Who could argue', as Rachels (1999: 98) observes, 'with the proposition that we should oppose suffering and promote happiness?' But he goes on to say:

> Yet in their own way Bentham and Mill were leading a revolution as radical as either of the other two great intellectual revolutions in the 19th century, those of Marx and Darwin. To understand the radicalness of the Principle of Utility, we have to appreciate what it leaves out of its picture of morality: Gone are all references to God or to abstract moral rules 'written in the heavens'. Morality is no longer to be understood as faithfulness to some divinely given code, or some set of inflexible rules. The point of morality is seen as the happiness of beings in this world, and nothing more; and we are permitted – even required – to do everything possible to promote that happiness. (1999: 98)

It is difficult to see how responsible decision making in social work could ever be carried out without a utilitarian element. Assuming that social workers intervene in people's lives in the hope of making things better, then it must surely be the case that we need to look at the likely consequences of an intervention to know whether it is justified. It is hard to see how an intervention could be considered ethical if all the evidence suggested that it would make things worse for everyone involved. It is hard to see, too, how we could justify doing something in a costly and time-consuming way, if it could be done just as well in a cheaper way that could save resources for use on other services. One of the benefits of a utilitarian approach, as opposed to a purely deontological one, is that it allows us to weigh up different courses of action in a situation where, however hard we try, we cannot necessarily do everything or help everyone. (Knowing that you have a duty to do a thing is not much help if you simply lack the means to put that duty into effect.)

But, though we can all agree that it is wrong to do something that will almost certainly make things worse, is it necessarily always *right* to do something that will make things better? If so, that would suggest that we should be entitled to intervene in other people's lives as much as we want, even against their wishes, if we can reasonably show that this will improve things for the greater number of people. This could lead to a very controlling and interventionist approach, in which there would be less and less room for people to make their own choices and their own mistakes.

A particular problem with a purely utilitarian approach is that the principle of the greatest good for the greatest number also carries with it the implication that it is acceptable to sacrifice the well-being of one person for the sake of the well-being of many. Torture is outlawed in most Western countries, but in the atmosphere of fear that followed the 9/11 attack on the World Trade Centre in New York, voices could be heard in government and the media, in the USA and the UK, arguing that the torture of terrorists might sometimes be justified if lives could be saved as a result. (And in fact, the USA, with the complicity of the UK, put this into effect when it used the device of 'extraordinary rendition' to get round its own legal restrictions by sending terrorist suspects to countries where these restrictions did not apply [BBC News, 2008; *The Guardian*, 2011].) But what are the limits to such an argument? Suppose the terrorist himself could not be captured, but his child was found – would it be justifiable to torture the child, in order to get the terrorist to give himself up and reveal the location of a bomb?

A calculation based solely on the greatest good of the greatest number would seem to justify such a decision, but we would guess that most people regard some actions as being simply beyond the pale in any circumstances, and would explain their position by appealing to something resembling Kant's categorical imperative. A human being cannot be used purely as a means to an end, they would argue, even if this would benefit a lot of other human beings. To give a social work example, to help a single very troubled young person may require the provision of very costly services (a therapeutic residential unit, for instance, may cost many thousands of pounds per week). The money used might be able to help large numbers of families. But does this entitle us to simply abandon a single troubled teenager to his fate?

ACT UTILITARIANISM AND RULE UTILITARIANISM

Some of the difficulties with the utilitarian approach can be addressed by moving from 'act utilitarianism' to 'rule utilitarianism'. As originally proposed by Bentham (1781), the rightness or wrongness of each action is determined by its utility (that is, its consequences). In practice, though, it is often difficult to know what the consequences of an individual action will be, and it is particularly difficult to know what the wider long-term consequences will be. In 'rule utilitarianism', the principle of utility is used, not to determine the rightness or wrongness of each individual action, but to generate rules of conduct. 'Individual acts are then determined to be right or wrong by the rules that, according to these evaluations, are the right rules for human beings to follow' (Deigh, 2010: 111).

Using this approach, we can, for instance, construct a utilitarian argument *against* using torture, even in the extreme situation described above, where to do so might possibly save lives. Even if a situation arose, this argument would go, in which torturing a captured terrorist to get information might prevent more suffering than it caused, in the long run we would still all benefit more from a complete ban on torture. This is because if we made a rule that torture could be used in some circumstances, it would mean that torture could easily end up being used in more and more cases, to the long-term detriment of a free and humane society with all the many benefits that brings to everyone. James Rachels calls this sort of reasoning 'The Slippery Slope Argument' (1999: 14), and we suspect that you will often come across situations in social work where, even if a given action might seem to be justified as a one-off decision, it becomes more problematic when you begin to think of the precedent it would set.

You may notice, incidentally, that a rule utilitarian model seems to have something in common with Kant's 'act only on that maxim whereby you can at the same time will that it become a universal law', and it may often result in similar conclusions. Nevertheless, the starting points of the two ideas are very different ones. Kant's approach starts with the categorical imperative. Rule utilitarianism works on the basis that what matters is the consequence of a given rule.

Before moving on to look at other approaches to ethical decision making, you may like to use the following exercise to look at how the different kinds of ethical reasoning that we've discussed so far – deontological and consequentialist – might be used in relation to an issue in social work.

THE BUDGET CUTS IN GREYSHIRE

Greyshire Children's Social Care Service is required by its local authority to cut its budget by 20%, because of reduced funding from central government. The Director of Children's Services has called a meeting of his social work staff to discuss the implications of this, and in particular to discuss how the budget cuts should be distributed. Should she cut back on services, such as child protection teams, which respond to emergency situations in which children may be acutely at risk, or should she make the cuts in family support services that help to prevent situations from becoming emergencies in the first place? (We don't know if many directors would really consult their staff to this extent, but let us suppose so for the sake of this exercise!)

EXERCISE 2.2

(Cont'd)

One social worker, Richard, argues that child protection work has got to be the priority:

'If it's a choice,' he says, 'our first duty has got to be to ensure the safety of children acutely at risk.'

Janice strongly disagrees:

'Our first duty is to the struggling families of Greyshire, and if we don't continue to offer support and advocacy for them, we'll become just another threat for them to fear.'

David agrees with Janice that supportive services should be maintained:

'I really think,' he says, 'that in the long run we may protect more children by offering support and advocacy to parents than we do by going in like firefighters when the situation has already gone too far.'

Lucy thinks he's wrong:

'Given the fact that our support and advocacy services are already quite small, I doubt that they really do all that much to prevent child protection situations arising. Don't get me wrong, it would be great to have a preventative approach to child abuse, but we just aren't adequately resourced for it even now. I think we should focus our limited resources on those most acutely at risk in order to make as much difference as possible.'

What do you notice about the arguments used by Richard, Janice, Lucy and David?

Comments on Exercise 2.2

Richard and Lucy argue in favour of concentrating on child protection services, but you may have noticed that they don't use the same type of argument. Richard argues in terms of duties, but Lucy's argument is to do with the most effective way of deploying resources.

Similarly, while both Janice and David argue in favour of supportive services, they also do not use the same argument as one another. Even though she disagrees with Richard, Janice argues, as he does, in terms of duties which cannot simply be set aside. David, however, uses an argument which is more like Lucy's, even though he comes to the opposite conclusion. Like Lucy, he sees the decision in terms of a pragmatic calculation as to which course of action will bring the greater benefit.

So, in terms of their positions on how to apply the cuts, Richard and Lucy take one side, while Janice and David take the other. But, in terms of the approach they take to determining what is right and what is wrong, we could pair Richard and Janice, on the one hand, and Lucy and David on the other. They don't use these words, but Richard's and

Janice's approaches are more deontological, while David's and Lucy's are more conse-quentialist and utilitarian.

You might like to consider what position you would take in a debate like this. However, for the purposes of this chapter, we would particularly like you to consider what approach you are more inclined to take when thinking about questions of right or wrong – deontological or consequentialist? Or perhaps you don't like either approach? If so, per-haps a 'virtue' perspective would be more to your taste.

VIRTUES

Let us be honest, if we were to ask you whether a person of your acquaintance – let's call him Karl – struck you as being a good person, you would be unlikely to say, 'Yes he is, because he always does his duty'. Nor would you say, 'Yes he is, because he always works out the consequences of everything he does, and makes sure he only does the thing that has the best outcome for most people'. More likely you would say something like: 'Yes he is, because he is brave, loyal, generous and kind'. In other words, your view on whether or not Karl is a good person would be based on your estimation of his virtues (and on their opposite, his vices) rather than on an analysis of the principles of action that he applies.

There is another whole approach to ethical questions which is neither deontologi-cal or consequentialist, but is based on the idea of virtues, or human qualities. It is particularly associated with Plato and Aristotle, Greek philosophers who lived nearly two and a half millennia ago, and, according to John Deigh, it was 'the dominant theory in ancient Greek ethics' (2010: 56). To describe this form of ethical think-ing, Deigh uses the term 'eudaimonism', which comes from a Greek word meaning 'flourishing', and refers to the idea that the right way for a person to act is the way that will tend to lead to their thriving and flourishing as a human being. The term 'virtue ethics' is usually used to describe modern developments in this area, which have enjoyed something of a revival in recent years as a reaction against approaches which seem to reduce ethical decision making to the rather dry and abstract business of weighing up principles and applying rules.

Promoting ethical practice, in this view, is more a matter of developing virtues than of learning how to analyse ethical dilemmas. According to Aristotle, virtues were habits of behaviour that struck a happy medium between extremes. *Courage*, for instance, is a virtue; *cowardice* is a vice resulting from lack of courage; and *reck-lessness* is a vice resulting from an excess of courage. A courageous person, from this perspective, is likely to live a fuller and better life, than either a cowardly one or a reckless one. In a modern application of the idea of virtues to professional ethics, Sarah Banks and Ann Gallagher suggest that 'virtue concepts (such as "trustworthi-ness" or "courage") consist of complex sets of dispositions to think, feel and act in certain ways in certain situations' (2009: 40).

VIRTUE ARGUMENTS IN GREYSHIRE

In Exercise 2.2, social workers offered deontological and consequentialist arguments for concentrating resources on child protection services or for protecting supportive services. Suppose that two other social workers also join in, Kim on the side of supportive services, and Danny on the side of child protection services, who both use arguments based on virtues. What sort of arguments might they offer?

Comments on Exercise 2.3

You may well have come up with completely different ideas, and referred to different virtues, but here are some suggestions:

Kim might argue that, if the team cuts back on supportive services in favour of concentrating solely on child protection work, 'we will deteriorate as social workers. We will become more punitive and suspicious and authoritarian. If we are to continue to be good, honest, caring social workers, we need to strike a balance between our investigatory, policing role and our supportive, helpful, listening role'.

So Kim is arguing for balance (the root of all virtues, if Aristotle is right) and for the need to maintain the virtues of kindness, openness and humility. This, rather than talk about duties or consequences, is the basis of her argument.

As for Danny, well perhaps he could argue that 'If we keep trying to offer our current level of supportive services when there is child protection work being left undone, we will not be being honest with ourselves. We claim that we are here first and foremost to protect children, and yet here we are saying that we will leave some children less well protected in order to allow ourselves to carry on doing something that we find easier and less uncomfortable than child protection work'.

You may or may not agree with Danny that it is being dishonest to put supportive services in front of child protection work, but the point here is that he is basing his argument on the virtue of 'honesty'.

Banks and Gallagher suggest that virtue ethics should not necessarily be seen as 'a comprehensive ethical theory covering all aspects of professional ethical life', but that 'consideration of the moral qualities of individual practitioners is a central part of any study of ethics' (2009: 39), and we would concur with this view. Useful and interesting as it can be to engage in seminar discussions of ethical dilemmas, this kind of intellectual activity will not in itself lead to students becoming good practitioners unless they also possess or develop qualities such as courage, integrity and respectfulness. Such qualities are not acquired by solving puzzles. Banks and Gallagher talk about the business of developing virtues such as courage as 'emotional work' (2009: 65). Julia Annas speaks of acquiring a virtue as being like acquiring a skill:

> It requires time, experience and habituation to develop it, but the result is not routine but the kind of actively and intelligently engaged mastery that we find in practical experts such as pianists and athletes. (Annas, 2011: 14)

THE ETHICS OF CARE

The term 'ethics of care' is used to describe an approach to thinking about ethics which is feminist in origin and which can be traced back to Carol Gilligan's influential book, *In a Different Voice* (1993). It would be misleading to suggest that this approach is in some way an offshoot of virtue ethics, because that was not Gilligan's starting point, but we think it would be true to say that this approach has a good deal in common with the kind of virtue-based approaches that we have just been discussing, for two reasons. First, it questions whether ethical questions should necessarily be looked at in terms of abstract duties or consequentialist calculations. Second, it is based on the idea that what lies at the core of moral behaviour are not rules of conduct but human qualities, in this case specifically the quality of being *caring*. (Exponents of the ethics of care, such as Virginia Held [2007] would view the idea of 'caring' as being a quality that applies to a *relationship*, though, rather than as a purely individual quality, or virtue.)

Gilligan's starting point, based on her own empirical observations, was a critique of theories of moral development which, in her view, gave precedence to a distinctively male way of thinking about moral questions. Her suggestion, as the title of the book indicates, was that women tend to think about moral questions in a way that is distinctive and different, but which had hitherto been devalued. (We say 'tend to' because Gilligan is careful not to suggest that *all* women think in one way, and *all* men in another.)

She proposed that girls and women tend to define themselves in terms of their connections with, and responsibilities to, other people, whereas boys and men tend to define themselves in terms of autonomy and separateness. Women's tendency to assume responsibility for taking care of others, leads women 'to attend to voices other than their own and to include in their judgement other points of view' (Gilligan, 1993: 16). From a narrowly rational and stereotypically male point of view, this flexibility may seem like vagueness, inconsistency or weakness, but it is, Gilligan argues, 'inseparable from women's moral strength, an overriding concern with relationships and responsibilities' (1993: 16–17). As Koggel and Orme sum up:

> In contrast to accounts of universal principles and of the significance of impartiality, individual rights, consequences, and justice in consequentialist and deontological moral theories, the ethic of care emphasizes the importance of context, interdependence, relationships, and responsibilities to concrete others. (2010: 109)

In the imaginary scenario described in Exercises 2.2 and 2.3, let us suppose that another social worker, Anne, steps into the discussion. Perhaps she works in a family centre of some kind.

'You're all talking here about this as if it were an abstract problem,' she says. 'The fact is that those of us who are providing supportive services to families have made a personal commitment to the people we work with. They aren't just "service users", they are Jane and Lisa, Abdul and Bill, Maria and Tina. We have a relationship with them, and they know we care about and are committed to them. You can't just simply pick up and discard human relationships, just because something else has supposedly become a higher priority. We have responsibilities to *these particular people*.'

She is speaking about the virtues of caring and loyalty, of course, but she is also talking in terms of her particular connections with specific real people. And it seems to us that there can be no doubt that this is indeed a vital and important aspect of ethical discourse. The difficulty with being caring in a professional sphere such as social work, is that it places workers in a position where they are required to care for people who are not part of their own informal caring networks (friends, children, parents, siblings, neighbours), but are people who they may meet only for a short time, in very specific contexts. When 'social care' may be accessed via a call centre, rationed out using needs assessment forms and eligibility criteria, defined by a 'care plan' and delivered as a 'care package' by several different 'care agencies', it can be difficult to remember the essentially personal nature of human care. But is it really possible to construct an ethical approach that leaves this dimension out?

We do however see some problems in an approach based exclusively on 'context, interdependence, relationships, and responsibilities to concrete others', in that it would seem to legitimate our natural tendency to care more for those we know, like or have a relationship with, than we care about strangers. In some ways, this very tendency is part of the problem for many users of social work services, who for one reason or another find themselves outside of the informal caring networks that sustain most of us.

STRUCTURE AND POWER

Let us now imagine that yet another social worker speaks up in the meeting described in Exercises 2.2 and 2.3.

'This whole exercise is nonsense,' says Ramona to the Director of Children's Services, expressing a view that some politically minded readers may have already formed. 'These cuts are not our responsibility. They are the result of debts the government incurred when it was trying to resolve a problem with the international banking system, debts which the government is now trying to reduce by cutting services to the most vulnerable people in our society. Don't try to push on to us the choice between child protection and family support. Both are needed, and if the government wants to cut one of them, then it will have to take the consequences. The message from everyone in this room should be that we refuse to choose because both kinds of service are vital. In fact we will fight to defend both of them. And you as director should be making clear to the council that if both services are not adequately funded, families will suffer and our agency will be unable to meet its basic legal obligations to them.'

What is important to Ramona is that the council and the public should receive a clear message about whose decision this really is and what has made the decision necessary in the first place. As far as she is concerned, the debate about the rights and wrongs of cutting one or other part of the service is a distraction from the real issue, which is that cuts will result in children suffering and the service failing to meet its legal obligations to provide both protective and preventative services. In other words, she is trying to move the argument away from the rights and wrongs of this particular issue to the structural and political questions that lie behind it. Her position is a radical one. The origin of this word (like that of the word 'radish') lies in the Latin word for 'root'. It means getting to the root of things.

Ramona's position is not so much a completely separate approach to the others described in this chapter, as a recognition that moral questions have more than one level to them, and it is often dishonest to deal with them in isolation without also looking at the political and social context, for the context often shapes and distorts the terms of the debate. In particular, structural inequality in society – the huge differences in power and wealth enjoyed by different sections of society – can seriously skew discussions about right and wrong.

It is generally agreed, for instance, that it is wrong to steal, and this makes it morally wrong to shoplift an item worth a few pence from a department store. And yet it is not generally considered morally wrong for a wealthy person to accumulate for his own personal use millions or billions of pounds which otherwise could be used to save hundreds or thousands of lives. (After all, many thousands die across the world every year for want of food or simple medicines, that might only cost a few pounds or even pence.) Is this not a rather one-sided kind of morality? This sort of thought led the nineteenth-century anarchist Pierre-Joseph Proudhon, in a book published in 1840, to ask the question 'What is property?' and give his own answer: 'Property is theft!' (Proudhon, 1994: 14).

There are many other examples of the way in which accepted standards of right and wrong are skewed in favour of the wealthy and powerful. Consider how much more indulgent a view society takes of tax evasion – a crime of the relatively well-off – than it does of benefit fraud, a crime of the poor. Or how, in societies where formal power is mainly or entirely held by men, a much more serious view is taken of female adultery and promiscuity than of male adultery and promiscuity. (You can probably easily think of half a dozen negative, value-laden terms that can be used for women who 'sleep around', but it is difficult to think of even one such word that can be used for promiscuous men.) Or think of the way in which, in nineteenth-century America, atrocities committed by Native Americans against white people were taken as evidence of their 'savage' nature and unfitness to run their own affairs, while the many atrocities committed by white people against Native Americans were not taken as evidence of the savagery of whites, or of their unfitness to govern themselves.

The classic formulation of the view that values, including morality, are the product of the power relations in a particular society, is that of Karl Marx (1818–83). In *The*

Communist Manifesto, published in 1848, Marx and his collaborator Friedrich Engels rhetorically address the capitalist ruling class (the bourgeoisie) in the following terms:

> Your very ideas are but the outgrowth of bourgeois production and bourgeois property, just as your jurisprudence is but the will of your class made into a law for all, a will whose essential character and direction are determined by the economical conditions of existence of your class. (Marx and Engels, 2004 [1848]: 25–6)

As Michel Foucault pointed out, 'every society has its own regime of truth ... the types of discourse which it accepts and makes function as true' (Foucault, 1980: 131). And broadly speaking, those who are powerful are those who are able to dictate what is defined as 'true'. Consider the different weight that might be given, in a courtroom for example, to, say, the views of a consultant psychiatrist who proposes a medical explanation for a given behaviour and a social worker who offers a purely social explanation. Which 'truth' prevails, the 'medical' or the 'social' explanation, may well not be the result so much of the objective merits of either kind of explanation but rather of the relative power of the speaker and the relative power of the world view which he or she represents.

But, of course, while a social worker's view may not always prevail against that of a psychiatrist, a social worker is often much more powerful than a social work service user and may well be able to impose her own 'truth' – her 'professional opinion' – over the 'truth' of a service user. It is therefore necessary for social workers to keep asking themselves the following uncomfortable question: 'I may think I am doing the right thing and being helpful to my service users, but am I really being helpful to them, or am I actually contributing to their oppression?'

We will return to these matters in Chapter 4. For the moment, what we wish to emphasise is that, whether we consider ethical questions in terms of duties, consequences or virtues, it is important that we think about the wider context in which our decisions take place, and recognise that everyday conventional wisdom about what is right and wrong is a wisdom that has been shaped for us by power and wealth.

CHAPTER SUMMARY

This chapter has explored different philosophical approaches to thinking about ethical questions, including approaches based on duties and rights, approaches based on looking at consequences and approaches based on the idea of virtues or human qualities, including the quality of caring. We concluded with some observations about the need to include the structural and political dimension in thinking about these matters.

Of course, we do not suggest that scholarly debates about the relative merits of utilitarianism and deontology are a common occurrence in the normal working day of a social worker, but debates about what is the right thing to do *are* common and, if you look under the surface of these debates, you will find differences of view, not only about what is right and wrong in a given situation, but about the nature of right and wrong themselves. Social workers do take deontological and utilitarian positions, even if they do not use those words, and do advocate various kinds of virtue ethics, even if they never mention Aristotle. Likewise, though they may never have heard of Foucault, social workers do notice the way that power shapes, and is shaped by, the way that we view things and what we perceive as 'right' and 'true'. And, whether or not they refer to Marx, any thoughtful social worker becomes aware that issues to do with social structures do often hide behind what may seem on the surface to be purely personal questions.

Apart from the kinds of ideas discussed in this chapter, many people are guided in their thinking about right and wrong by religious beliefs. It is this that we consider in the next chapter.

FURTHER READING

The following book, cited in this chapter, provides a clear and interesting explanation of the application of virtue ethics to professional ethics in the helping professions:

Banks, S. and Gallagher, A. (2009) *Ethics in Professional Life*. Basingstoke: Palgrave.

The following text, cited several times in this chapter, provides a useful introduction to ethics as a subject of philosophical study. It is an introductory text, but it is aimed at students of philosophy, and is therefore rather more technical than the broad-brush introduction we have been able to offer here.

Deigh, J. (2010) *An Introduction to Ethics*. Cambridge: Cambridge University Press.

3
VALUES AND RELIGION

- Social work values and religion: historic links
- Recognising religious needs
- The multi-faith context
- Challenging religion
- Limits of the 'scientific' model
- Notes for practice

When a second edition of a textbook is being considered, publishers often commission reviews of the first edition, in order to identify areas that might benefit from changes. In the case of this book, reviewers made various helpful suggestions which we have tried to address in the present edition, but when it came to the present chapter, their views were sharply divided. Some identified its inclusion as a particular strength of the book, while others felt it should not have been included at all.

The two authors of this book do not have the same views on religion. One (Andrew) is a practising Christian. The other (Chris) is an atheist, or, at any rate, not an adherent of any particular organised religion. Nevertheless, both of us find it hard to understand how a book on values and ethics could be complete without a discussion of religion, for, as we noted in the previous chapter, religion is for many people the source of their values. (Indeed, we think it probable that this would be true of the great majority of people in the world today.) This is certainly true of many users of social work services, and it is true of too many social workers. For example, a 2003 survey of social work students at the University of Bradford found that 28% described themselves as Christian and 23% as Muslim, with 15% of students attending religious services on a regular basis (Gilligan and Furness, 2006). It is also the case that many of the founders of social work as a profession, as well as many of the oldest and most well-known social work agencies, had and still have a quite explicit religious value base.

What is more, social work is about meeting people's needs, and it cannot afford to ignore the fact that many people, even among those who are not religious in a formal sense, see 'spiritual needs' as being of central importance, or the fact that, for very large numbers of people, religion provides a means of meeting those spiritual needs. Indeed, British law and policy guidance *require* social workers to think about the religious needs of service users. For example, the 1989 Children Act (still the main legal framework for child and family social work in England and Wales) requires local authorities to give due consideration to a child's 'religious persuasion, racial origin and cultural and linguistic background' (Section 22 [5]).

YOUR POSITION ON RELIGION

Before going further, you may like to reflect on the following questions:

- What does religion mean to you? Do you subscribe to a particular religion? Were you brought up in one? What kinds of feelings do you have towards religion, positive, indifferent or hostile?
- How much would you say your beliefs about 'right' or 'wrong' are based upon religious teachings?
- How does your position on religion influence how you see others and the world we live in?
- How does it influence the way you see people who take a different view on religion to yourself?
- Do you find it difficult to talk about religion in a social work context? Would you want to?

EXERCISE 3.1

Comments on Exercise 3.1

We obviously cannot comment on what you may have come up with here. However, two thoughts that occur to us are these:

- These are very personal questions. Any two individuals – even two individuals who work together well and would agree on many other things – can turn out to have radically different views on religious questions. Indeed, as we have already noted, the two authors of this book are a case in point. It is a curious fact that two people can disagree profoundly on the fundamental nature of the universe, and yet work together quite satisfactorily on the problems thrown up by everyday life. But it is fortunate that this is so, because in any society (and especially in a multi-cultural one) each of us is surrounded by people who disagree with us on these fundamental questions.
- While it is quite possible for people with fundamental differences in religious beliefs to work together, it can be challenging. For example, some religious people believe

(Cont'd)

that only those who subscribe to their own faith will be saved from an eternal punishment. To other people, this can sound pretty much like saying 'The rest of you can
all go to hell' – and it can arouse strong negative feelings. Equally, some non-believers
are inclined to laugh at religion and dismiss it as ignorant superstition on a par,
say, with belief in Santa Claus or the tooth fairy. For religious people, whose beliefs
and religious practices form a profoundly important part of their lives, this can feel
extremely disrespectful and hurtful, and it can make people reluctant to bring up
their religious views for fear of ridicule. In fact, because of the potential for conflict
and uncomfortable feelings, discussion of religious differences – and the religious
dimension in people's lives – is very often avoided altogether.
- Simply to avoid the topic in this way, though, does not seem to us legitimate for social
  workers, who have to deal with people with many different religious backgrounds.

SOCIAL WORK VALUES AND RELIGION: HISTORIC LINKS

Social work values and practices are rooted in traditions which derived from Christian
or Judaeo-Christian discourse. Although expressed today in language which has deliberately foregone its Christian tone, social work is built on assumptions about individual
subjectivity, community and service to others which have a strong continuing presence
in Christian discourse. (Cree, 1995: 50)

Cree suggests that the Christian tradition created the foundations upon which the
modern social work profession's value base was laid. As a matter of historic record this
is surely, at least in part, the case. Social work as a distinct profession developed pri-
marily in Europe and North America, where Christianity is the dominant religious
tradition, and many of the agencies which originally pioneered what we would now
call social work were motivated quite specifically by Christian belief. Indeed, many of
them still are. For instance, if we take three of the UK's largest independent providers
of child welfare services: the Children's Society is an offshoot of the Church of England,
the National Children's Home has Methodist roots and Barnado's states on its website:

Barnardo's derives its inspiration and values from the Christian faith. Today we work in
a multi-cultural society, but we are proud of the Christian values and beliefs upon which
we were founded. (Barnado's, undated: online)

Thomas Barnado himself is one of a number of specifically Christian 'founding
fathers' of what we would now recognise as social work, and there are many emi-
nent 'founding mothers' too who were likewise motivated by their Christian faith,
among them Elizabeth Fry, Josephine Butler and Octavia Hill. Felix Biestek (1963),
who is widely quoted in books such as this one on social work values and remains

hugely influential, was a Roman Catholic priest. His code of ethics is rooted in a tradition of Christian ethics and theology, as much on any philosophical tradition, and certainly does not owe its origins to the social sciences upon which social work has traditionally drawn for its intellectual base. Terry Philpot (1986) argues that Biestek's principle of respect for persons cannot be 'derived from the social sciences at all, but is, in essence, a religious value, having its justification in a transcendental view of life' (Philpot, 1986: 143). (It is true that social sciences, on their own, cannot be expected to come up with answers to value questions. However, as we saw in the previous chapter, many would argue that respect for persons can be built on other bases than religion.)

Of the major religions, Christianity is not the only one that has been influential in social work. There are long-standing Jewish social work agencies. In Islam, the obligation to give help to those in need is a fundamental tenet of the faith, with *zakaah* (or *zakat*), the giving of alms, being the third of the five 'pillars of Islam'. Buddhism has been an influence in social work thinking, not only in predominantly Buddhist countries, but in Western countries too. (See, for instance, the work of our late colleague, David Brandon [1990, 2000], who was also interested in Taoism.) However, Christianity is almost certainly the most influential religion in the development of social work as a modern profession, perhaps because professional social work is something that emerged in the industrialised world and it was in the predominantly Christian West that the industrial revolution began. (The historical relationship between religion and social work in this country is explored by Philpot [1986] and Cree [1995].)

In view of the history and of the continuing links between religious faiths and social work agencies, it is interesting that talk about the relationship between social work and its Christian roots sometimes seems (in our experience) to create a certain unease in social work circles, as does talk about the 'spiritual' dimension of life generally. But even social workers who are confirmed atheists cannot avoid the fact that many of the roots of their own profession and its values go back to the Christian ethic of serving God through charity, an ethic which is shared by the other major religions. An atheist or humanist might wish to recast this ethic in terms that did not include the idea of a personal God – we might talk of empathy for others as being part of what it means to be human: a recognition of the fact that we are part of a greater whole – but the fact remains that many of the founders of social work would have cast it in its specifically religious form.

RECOGNISING RELIGIOUS NEEDS

Religion

'... the belief in and worship of a superhuman controlling power; especially a personal God or gods ... a particular system of faith and worship ...'. (*Oxford Dictionary of English*, 2009)

Whether or not social workers are motivated by religious faith, there can be no doubt that many of the people that they work with will be. For many people, belief in 'a supernatural controlling power' and in an afterlife, meets an important need. There is even some empirical evidence to suggest that subscribing to a religion can have beneficial effects on mental health (Kalish and Reynolds, 1976, for instance, found that people who had strong religious convictions had less anxiety about death, though atheists did better than people with confused and unclear religious beliefs). For many, religion also provides an important sense of *belonging*. Holding to a particular faith, and its attendant practices, is a crucial part of their identity.

Failure to recognise the importance of religion in the lives of service users can, at worst, amount to an attack on their sense of well-being, their integrity and their identity.

EXERCISE 3.2

SERVICE USERS' RELIGIOUS BELIEFS

Can you think of instances where failure to recognise the religious beliefs of a service user would result in basic needs going unmet?

Comments on Exercise 3.2

Here are two imaginary scenarios:

Mr Patel, an elderly Hindu man, is admitted to a residential home in an emergency, due to the hospitalisation of his carer. He is frightened and disorientated. All of the residents in the home are white British and the staff are either white British or black British of African-Caribbean origin. The staff in the home are proud of their cultural awareness and when it comes to meal times, they inform Mr Patel that they have gone to some trouble to provide pork-free meals made using halal meat. Some of the care staff seem to think they have already gone some way beyond the call of duty to meet what they are inclined to see as pernickety dietary foibles. Sensing this, Mr Patel does not feel able to tell them that in fact he is a Hindu, not a Muslim, and that his faith prohibits the eating not of pork but of beef, as the cow is a sacred animal in Hinduism. Many Hindus are completely vegetarian, in fact, though Mr Patel is not. But to eat food which might include beef feels to Mr Patel like an act of self-pollution, degradation and wickedness. Already feeling frightened, lost and deprived of the familiar environment which normally gives his daily life some structure and meaning, Mr Patel feels he has no choice but to decline food altogether. What seems a minor matter to non-religious people – or to people with different religious traditions – may for a religious person be a matter that goes deep to the core of their sense of self-worth and belonging.

Jane, aged 15, is a white British girl who has been temporarily accommodated away from her family in a foster home due to allegations made about a family member which suggest that she may be at risk at home. This is a very lonely and very fright-ening situation. Jane is an active member of an evangelical Christian church, and has derived a great deal of support both from the other members of the church and from the belief system which Christianity provides. It is important to her at times of difficulty to be able to pray and to be able to turn to other church members. However, the social worker who placed her here has not picked up on this dimension in Jane's life. Jane has experience of being ridiculed by her peers for her religious beliefs and she has already heard her foster-father (who is unaware of her religion) making disparaging comments about 'bible-bashers'. She is frightened to pray for fear of being discovered, and does not know how to go about asking to be allowed to contact her church. Jane is therefore cut off from sources of support which would help her through this difficult time.

THE MULTI-FAITH CONTEXT

Recognising and responding to religious needs is, of course, more challenging in a society in which many different religious traditions co-exist. Social workers need to understand how different faiths, in very different ways, help in maintaining and supporting their communities. They need to understand some of the dynamics of these diverse communities and apply their understanding to their practice. Indeed, the very nature of the relationship between an individual and a community is some-thing that may differ in different communities. In the Western, secular context, the importance of the individual may be seen as paramount. In some other communi-ties, the needs of the individual may come second to those of the community.

Thompson's (2006) PCS model may be helpful here. The model offers a straight-forward frame for looking at how inequalities and discrimination manifest and per-petuate themselves in 'the social circumstances of clients, and in the interactions between clients and the welfare state'. The model operates on three levels: the P level (personal or psychological), the C level (the cultural level: 'shared ways of seeing, thinking and doing' [Thompson, 2006: 27]) and the S level that relates to structural matters.

Let us now apply this specifically to religion. Beginning with the 'P' level and con-sidering what religion can mean for individual people, we can see that it can form the basis of some of the strongest emotions that people experience, and underpin attitudes and thought patterns which may govern and direct the life of the believer and form the cement that sustains and holds that follower in a particular way of life. Religion can be a great source of strength and integrity for an individual though, conversely, and as Thompson has recognised, strong beliefs can also produce inflex-ibility that may lead to prejudice.

Moving to the 'C' level, religion can and does provide for many people a sense of a shared belonging, a feeling of cohesion and membership of a family that unites believers and can, in some instances (though sadly not by any means in all), increase understanding or tolerance of the similar needs that are met by other faiths. In Islam, this community of believers is known as the *Ummah*, rather powerfully evoked in the following extract from a newspaper article:

> Ummah is sometimes defined as the community, sometimes the nation, sometimes the body of Muslim believers around the globe, and it has a physical reality, without parallel in any other religion, that is nowhere better expressed than in the five daily times of prayer.
>
> The observant believer turns to the Ka'aba in Mecca, which houses the great black meteorite said to be the remnant of the shrine given to Abraham by the angel Gabreel, and prostrates himself before Allah at Shorooq (sunrise), Zuhr (noon), Asr (mid-afternoon), Maghreb (sunset) and Isha (night). These times are calculated to the nearest minute, according to the believer's longitude and latitude, with the same astronomical precision required for sextant-navigation. (The crescent moon is the symbol of Islam for good reason: the Islamic calendar, with its dates for events like the Haj and Ramadan, is lunar, not solar.) Prayer times are published in local newspapers and can be found online, and for believers far from the nearest mosque, a $25 Azan clock can be programmed to do the job of the muezzin. So, as the world turns, the entire Ummah goes down on its knees in a never-ending wave of synchronised prayer, and believers can be seen as the moving parts of a universal Islamic chronometer (Raban, 2003).

But a similar sense of belonging is an important part of all religions. The Christian Bible, for instance, speaks of believers being 'one, as thou, Father, art in me, and I in thee, that they also may be one in us' (John 18: 21).

Finally, at the 'S' level, we can see many instances of organised religion being actively involved in striving to correct structural injustices (religious leaders were prominent both in the nineteenth-century campaign against slavery and in the twentieth-century struggle against apartheid, for instance) and in organised efforts to obviate the effects of oppression and discrimination. But we can also see ways that religion at this level can in itself be used for oppressive purposes (consider the oppression of women in the name of Islam in Afghanistan under the Taliban, or the torture and killings carried out in the name of Christianity by the Spanish Inquisition).

But it is the interplay *between* these three levels that is particularly subtle and complex. For instance, it may be that a specific set of religious beliefs may meet real and important needs both for a community and for individuals within that community, and yet at the same time perpetrate oppression at a structural level. Religious beliefs may simultaneously be both liberating and oppressive.

Incidentally, Bernard Moss proposes adding an additional 'S' to the PCS analysis, the 'S' signifying spirituality, suggesting that 'spirituality can be seen to an all encompassing dimension that is both affected by, and in its turn can affect, all the other components within the model' (2008: 61). Some non-religious readers in Western secularised societies may feel that this is overemphasising the spiritual, or religious level of experience, but there is no doubt that for many people across the world, religion is absolutely central to their experience. It may also be more important for some subgroups of the UK population that it is for the population as a whole. The 2001 Home Office Citizenship Survey asked a sample of UK citizens the question: 'Which of the following things would say something important about you, if you were describing yourself?' and found that 'religion', on average, came ninth after 'family', 'work', 'age', 'interests', 'education', 'nationality', 'gender' and 'income'. However, for black people it came third, after 'family' and 'ethnicity'. For Asian people, it came second after 'family', while Jewish respondents rated 'religion' first (O'Beirne, 2004). In this context, it is interesting how little emphasis is placed on religion in many social work courses, given the fact that considerable emphasis *does* tend to be placed on cultural sensitivity, and concerning that some students apparently feel the need to conceal or downplay their religious background in what Humphrey (2009: 8) describes as a 'faith closet'.

CHALLENGING RELIGION

Now, if it is important to respect religious beliefs, it is equally important to recognise that respect for religious beliefs should not be uncritical and cannot override all other factors in a given situation. There is a necessary tension between the need to recognise the importance of religion to people – even of religions whose basic tenets we ourselves may not agree with – and the need to be able to challenge where necessary. It is in striking this balance in the real world that difficulties start to appear. If respecting other people's value systems is part of our own value system, then what do we do in situations where other people's deeply held beliefs lead them to behave in ways which, within the frame of our own value system, are simply wrong? This is not so much of a problem when those involved are, so to speak, 'consenting adults', but it becomes a real dilemma where there are children involved or other people who may not be in a position to make their own choices.

For instance, both Islam and Judaism prescribe male circumcision – the removal of the foreskin of small boys – and this remains legal in the UK and other countries. In other circumstances, taking a knife to a small child and removing a part of his body without a medical reason would be seen as a serious assault, which would occasion intervention by child protection services. But here is an instance where respect for religious beliefs is generally accepted as 'trumping' the need to protect children from violence, for circumcision in both traditions is an important marker of belonging and, even if we are not Muslims or Jews, we know that belonging – a sense of identity – is an important human need. However, the question then arises as to where the limits would lie to what is acceptable in the name of religion. In the UK and elsewhere, the much more drastic procedure of *female* genital mutilation, for instance, is not legal, even though it is also accepted as normal and appropriate in many parts of the world, and could itself be claimed as a marker of identity and belonging.

The case of Victoria Climbié (Laming, 2003) who died in London in February 2000 at the hands of her great aunt Marie-Therese Kouao and her partner is an instance where religious belief played a destructive role. British readers will almost certainly be familiar with this high-profile case which has led to much heart searching within British society, but briefly the circumstances are that Victoria was a child from Côte d'Ivoire in West Africa who was sent by her parents to live with her aunt, first in France and then in London, in order to get a good education. A good education was never provided. Instead, Victoria was subjected to an appalling catalogue of cruelty leading to her death at the age of 8. Among the horrors to which she was subjected were being kept tied up in a black plastic bag containing her own excrement in an empty bath, and being forced to eat cold food placed in front of her on a piece of plastic.

Victoria's carers, we are informed in Chapter 3 of the Laming report (Laming, 2003), sought advice and guidance from churches as to how to deal with Victoria:

> ... On 29 August 1999, Kouao and Victoria attended the Mission Ensemble pour Christ ...

> The pastor here was Pascal Orome ... Kouao told him about Victoria's incontinence and he formed the view that she was possessed by an evil spirit. He advised that the problem could be solved by prayer.

> Two weeks after her first visit to his church, Kouao phoned Pastor Orome and told him that, following a brief improvement, Victoria's incontinence had returned. He claimed he reproached her for being insufficiently vigilant and allowing the spirit to return. (Laming, 2003: 32)

Later, shortly before her death, Kouao took Victoria to a church again:

> There is evidence to suggest that by 19 February 2000, Victoria was very ill. On this day, which was a Saturday, Kouao took her to the Universal Church of the Kingdom of God ... Audrey Hartley-Martin, who was assisting Pastor Alvaro Lima in the administration of the 3 pm service, noticed the two of them coming up the stairs. They were shouting at each other and Victoria seemed to be having difficulty walking.

> Kouao and Victoria were disturbing the service, so Ms Hartley-Martin took Victoria downstairs to the crèche. She noticed Victoria was shivering and asked if she was cold. Victoria replied that she was not cold but she was hungry. Ms Hartley-Martin obtained some biscuits for her ... she did not seek to ensure Victoria received any medical attention because she 'was not aware that the child was ill'.

> At the end of the service, Pastor Lima spoke to Kouao about the difficulties she said she was having with Victoria, particularly her incontinence. He expressed the view that Victoria's problems were due to her possession by an evil spirit and said he would spend the week fasting on Victoria's behalf. He believes he made it clear that Victoria was not expected to fast herself... (Laming, 2003: 35)

These churches were only two out of many different bodies which failed to recognise the seriousness of Victoria's plight. However, by constructing Victoria's problems as something within herself – 'possession by an evil spirit' – they played a profoundly unhelpful role. First, it seems likely that by allowing her aunt to see Victoria as a person possessed by an evil spirit (rather than as a very unhappy little girl – and latterly as a very ill little girl), the church inadvertently helped to legitimate the catalogue of physical abuse and mental cruelty to which she was subjected. Second, blinded by their own 'spiritual' explanations for what was happening, the churches failed to see what was really going on until it was too late. When Kouao reported that Victoria had been unconscious for two days and had neither eaten nor drunk anything, Pastor Lima did eventually advise that she should go to hospital. She was admitted to the North Middlesex Hospital and then moved to St Mary's Hospital Paddington, where, in spite of medical intervention, she was to die, suffering from severe hypothermia and multi-system failure, with injuries so extensive that one doctor said they were 'too numerous' to record.

CHALLENGING RELIGIOUS BELIEFS

EXERCISE 3.3

Thinking about the involvement of the churches in the Victoria Climbié case, what general lessons do you think social workers could draw about their response to explanations for events based on religious beliefs, and what dangers are there to be avoided?

Comments on Exercise 3.3

Among the lessons that we would draw from this story are that respect for other people's religious beliefs cannot be extended to the point of failing to challenge 'spiritual' explanations for events which seem to have other causes, or religious justifications for behaviour which would seem to be likely to cause harm. It is important to guard against the danger of failing to challenge for fear of offending religious sensibilities.

This is easy to say, but harder to put into practice. As we have already shown, using the case of male circumcision as an illustration, even behaviour and beliefs which, from the point of view of a non-believer, are harmful may need to be tolerated and accepted in recognition of a bigger picture in which these behaviours or beliefs provide benefits to the individuals involved as well as immediate harm. So, although there is a danger of failing to challenge, there is also an opposite danger of challenging practices and beliefs without understanding the wider context.

Clearly in the case of Victoria Climbié, there was no wider context in this sense. There was no sense in which she could be said to have benefited from being seen as possessed by evil spirits. In a situation of this kind, it is surely clear that the duty to protect vulnerable individuals from harm must take precedence over the duty to respect religious beliefs.

In the long-run, what seems to be needed too, though, is for professional agencies to build links with churches and other religious organisations, both at the local level and at a structural level, so that there is more trust and more understanding of each other's perspectives. As we have seen, Pastor Lima did eventually take steps to get Victoria to hospital, but it was too late. Perhaps if he had had better links with local professional agencies, he would have felt able to involve them at an earlier stage.

LIMITS OF THE 'SCIENTIFIC' MODEL

A social work curriculum that deletes or omits content related to the spiritual dimension may be called 'hollow'. (Sollod, 1992: 60)

Having criticised the churches in the Victoria Climbié case for allowing themselves to be blinded by 'spiritual' explanations, it seems appropriate to balance this by noting that the 'spiritual' dimension is important in thinking about human life, and that it is possible too to be 'blinded by science'.

In the second half of the twentieth century, social work came increasingly under the influence of models of human behaviour derived from the social sciences, which offer explanations for human behaviour in terms which emulate those of the natural sciences. Freudian psychology and its various off-shoots is one example. Psychodynamic theories emulate the physical sciences by attempting to explain human behaviour in terms of a dynamic interaction of forces. Behaviourism is another example, as is, in its way, Marxism. These may seem very different to one another, but what they do have in common is a degree of determinism: the assumption that a person is the product of circumstances, and that we can explain why a person behaves in a given way in terms of various mechanisms, rather in the way that (say) an astronomer can explain the movements of planets and stars by calculating the interplay of momentum and gravitational forces, or a chemist can explain the properties of different substances in terms of the properties of atoms and molecules. It can be useful to look at things in this way and it is certainly not our intention here to discredit the social sciences, though it is important to note that none of the three approaches mentioned has anything *like* the same predictive precision that can be achieved in chemistry or astronomy.

What we want to note, though, is that this way of looking at people is necessarily a *partial* view. There is a danger, if we only look at things in this 'scientific' way, that we will begin to see the users of our services as mere passive recipients of 'help', with the social worker, alongside other practitioners of the human sciences, as a technocratic expert whose job it is to 'fix' defective lives as a mechanic fixes defective engines. This is not an appropriate model for at least two reasons. First, as we have already noted, it is inappropriate because nothing *like* this level of expertise exists in the human sciences, where the ability to predict and explain is at best limited, and where theories and models are almost all matters of discussion and dispute. Second, it is not appropriate because it is demeaning to the users of services to cast them as the products of their environment and history, rather than as the free agents that we assume ourselves to be.

Even some of the more 'radical' and less 'scientific' modern formulations of the social work role may be guilty of this tendency to deny agency to service users if they construct users of social work services merely as victims of social injustices and misfortunes of various kinds, without balancing this with a view of service users as moral beings making their own moral choices. There is a germ of truth in the tabloid stereotype of the social worker as a person who makes excuses for bad behaviour. (The magazine *Punch* once printed a cartoon of Genghis Khan riding out to pillage and slaughter with an earnest social worker on the horse behind him, all too ready to explain away his actions in terms of childhood trauma and a broken home.)

There is surely a point at which attempting to understand the reasons for some-one's actions crosses over into denying them the right to take responsibility for them-selves. One of us has noted elsewhere, for instance, that if we accept that some residential social workers may be guilty of the crime of abusing children in their care, then we must also accept that some former care residents may be guilty of the no greater crime of making false allegations of abuse. To suggest that only *we* are capable of evil and that service users are only capable of being *victims* of evil is, in a curious way, demeaning to service users (Beckett, 2002).

But science – and, by extension, social science – are necessarily in the business of *explanations*, which is why they are not of much help with value questions and can obscure the fact that, as a matter of practical necessity, human beings must see themselves as making their own choices as they move through life. Holland (1989) observes that, while the profession

> has drawn heavily upon various theories of human development, it has paid little atten-tion to the processes and contents of the moral and spiritual dimensions of human expe-rience. Too often we have examined human relationships and social issues not as moral and spiritual issues, but rather as technical matters to be understood in terms of refined psycho-social theory and empirical research. (Holland, 1989: 35)

It seems to us that, while it is important to look for explanations – and important to recognise that human beings are, in a sense, products of their environment – it is also important to simultaneously hold in mind a view of people as free to make choices. And for such a perspective we have to look elsewhere than the social sci-ences. There are a number of places we could look for alternative models. We could look at existentialist philosophy, for instance, or at Carl Rogers' person-centred approach (Rogers, 1967). But another place to look is in any one of the major reli-gious traditions, all of which have, for centuries, constructed the human individual as an active agent, a moral being, making choices between good and evil, right and wrong. We return to the theme of choice in Chapter 8.

NOTES FOR PRACTICE

We will conclude this chapter with a few brief notes on good practice with reference to religious beliefs.

- Developing a genuinely comprehensive picture of people, their needs and their strengths must include consideration of the role that religious or other belief systems play in their lives. The picture would be seriously incomplete without such consideration and it would be contrary to the basic principle of respect, to attempt an assessment without looking at what is important to the service user, or how the service user sees and interprets the world.
- In practice, this requires that social workers make it their business to acquire a working knowledge of different religious traditions, as and when they encounter them. Of course, it also requires recognition that religion is not homogeneous: the beliefs of one Christian are

not necessarily the same as the beliefs of another Christian; the beliefs of one Muslim are not necessarily those of every Muslim. And many people have idiosyncratic beliefs and value systems which cannot be neatly pigeonholed into the categories of established religious faiths.

- Failure to recognise the religious dimension in people's lives can not only result in important needs going unmet, it can also result in behaviour being misinterpreted. Andrew is reminded of a story about a black woman who was thought to be schizophrenic because she was speaking apparent gibberish into thin air. In actual fact, the woman was praying in a dialect that was unfamiliar to the psychiatrist and those carrying out the assessment.
- Regardless of whether or not we share a person's religious beliefs, or find those beliefs personally convincing or appealing, it is important to recognise that such beliefs are for many people the bedrock on which they construct meaning and purpose in their lives, and the means by which they make sense of value questions (the very kind of questions which this book explores).
- However, this is not to say that an uncritical acceptance of all beliefs and practices prescribed by different religions is required. As we have demonstrated, there are circumstances in which other factors must take priority.

CHAPTER SUMMARY

In this chapter, we have considered the role that religion has played as a source of meaning and as a reference point for value questions, both in life generally, and in social work in particular.

We have noted that religion played an important role in the development of social work as a profession, insofar as many of its founders were motivated by religious beliefs, and we have noted that in the present day a substantial proportion of those who go into social work are similarly motivated. We have noted that religion will have an absolutely key role in the lives of many service users, and that it is important that these needs are recognised alongside the other kinds of needs which social workers include in their assessments, and we have considered the challenges of doing this in a multi-faith context. We have also emphasised, using the case of Victoria Climbié as an example, that supposedly religious practices do sometimes need to be challenged if they are being used as a pretext to harm vulnerable people.

 ## FURTHER READING

The following, by authors we have cited in this chapter, is one of relatively few recent books to have specifically addressed the relationship between religion and social work:

Furness, S. and Gilligan, P. (2010) *Religion, Belief and Social Work*. Bristol: Policy Press.

See also the following book by Bernard Moss whose work we have cited here as well:

Moss, B. (2005) *Religion and Spirituality*. Lyme Regis: Russell House.

4
VALUES AND POLITICS

- The political dimension of social work
- Dealing with politics
- Social work, radicalism and social change

Questions about what is right and what is wrong are not confined to the personal sphere. We speak of laws, institutions and social structures, not just individuals, as being just or unjust, and when we discuss politics, we talk in terms of right and wrong, just as we talk about right and wrong in our personal lives. Politics is not the same thing as ethics, but it is one of the areas in which ethical questions arise and it cannot simply be bracketed out of ethical debates. 'The realms of ethics and politics can be neither divided nor conflated', argues the literary theorist Terry Eagleton:

> Ethics deal with such questions as human values, purposes, relationships, qualities of behaviour, motives for action, while politics raises the question of what material conditions, power-relations and social institutions we need in order to foster certain of these values and qualities but not others. (Eagleton and Beaumont, 2009: 301)

For the rest of this chapter, we will discuss the implications for social work of this inevitable overlap between politics and ethics, but before going any further, the reader may like to consider his or her own political position.

YOUR POLITICAL VALUES

We have included this exercise because not everyone has clearly defined political views, and many people do not align themselves with a particular political party or a particular political ideology. However, it is going to be argued in this chapter that we have a responsibility

(Cont'd)

EXERCISE 4.1

to think about our political values and obligations as well as our personal ones, so it seems appropriate to ask you to try and identify your own political stance. Consider which, out of each of the following pairs of statements, you agree with more, and then think why. What does your answer say about your values?

1   (a) I think that the state should spend more on public services, funded by an increase in taxation on the better-off. *Or:* (b) I think that taxation should be reduced, and public spending cut accordingly.

2   (a) I think anyone who wants to enter the country should be allowed to do so, unless they present a real immediate danger. *Or:* (b) I think restrictions on immigration to this country should either continue as at present or be stricter than at present.

3   (a) I think the capitalist system, for all its faults, is the best available economic model. *Or:* (b) I think the capitalist system, in which the world economy is dominated by privately owned corporations, is fundamentally unjust and should be replaced by ... (what)?

4   (a) I think the criminal justice system is too soft on criminals. *Or:* (b) I think the criminal justice system is too punitive.

COMMENTS ON EXERCISE 4.1

What we wish you to notice here is the value base on which your choices are made.

For example, if, in response to (1) you opted for (a), your view was presumably based on a belief that fairness requires the wealth of a country to be spread around and not concentrated in the hands of a few. If you opted for (b), on the other hand, and you take the view that people should be allowed to keep more of the money they themselves earn, this might be for one of two reasons. You may feel that it is a necessary incentive to hard work (and therefore good for the economy, and therefore perhaps ultimately good even for the less well-off). You may simply feel that it is just and fair that people should be allowed to keep most of what they earn, even if this does mean less money for public services. There are two very different conceptions of 'fairness' here, one concerned with sharing, the other more concerned with allowing people to benefit from their own actions. We suggest that your own particular understanding of what fairness is (which may well be reflected by your choices in pair (4) also) will have a significant bearing on the approach you take to service users.

Similarly, if you chose (a) out of the second pair of statements, you would probably explain your view in terms of common humanity or universal human rights. (Why shouldn't people live where they want to live? Why should people from poor countries be prevented from seeking a better life in rich ones?). But if you chose (b), you might have offered a number of different arguments. You might feel that the main obligations of a nation state are to its own citizens. (If that is your view, you are perhaps less taken with the idea of universal human rights, and more taken with the idea of rights as a sort of contract between citizens and the state.) You might feel that a state needs to maintain a degree of stability and cohesion and that this might be threatened if there was a very large scale of people from other parts of the world. (If that is your view, you are effectively saying that community cohesion or stability is sometimes more important than individual rights.) Again, the particular stance you take is likely to affect your approach to your work, and may affect your decisions in particular practice contexts, as will be discussed below.

You choice for pair (3) will most likely reflect the way you view the issues to be considered in this chapter, for social work, as it now functions, is the creation of a particular type of society. The extent to which you feel able to go along with social work as it now exists, will probably reflect the extent to whether you see modern society as something that is in need of reform, or something that needs to be replaced by a different social structure. Certainly, under capitalism, huge differences in wealth and power exist, and most social work service users are at the poor and powerless end of the spectrum.

THE POLITICAL DIMENSION OF SOCIAL WORK

Social work is a political creation. The problems and challenges with which social workers deal are themselves the products of a particular political context, and social work is a particular kind of public response to them, created in very large part by the state, either directly or through grants paid to voluntary or private organisations. In fact, it is impossible to envisage social work existing as a distinct profession at all, except as the product of politics:

> All social work, to count as such, is authorised and legitimated as a result of public and political processes ... this remains true even in those regimes where the delivery of social work services is delegated to non-state organisations. (Clark, 2000: 4)

This means that when you practise as a social worker, you will be implementing policies and ways of working that have come about because of political decisions. You will not always agree with them, just as you will not always agree with other kinds of political decision; you may wonder whether they are ethical; you may sometimes feel that they are oppressive, or likely to make things worse for service users rather than better. At times, too, you may even feel that the policies you are asked to implement are dishonest, for new policies and initiatives can sometimes amount to nothing much more than symbolic gestures to reassure the public. Political initiatives may even serve purposes which are different from, or even opposite to, their ostensible objectives, as memorably satirised in George Orwell's famous novel *Nineteen Eighty-Four* (2004 [1949], in which the true purpose of the Ministry of Peace was to wage perpetual war, and the true purpose of the Ministry of Truth was to tell lies. Just because an agency describes itself as 'person-centred' or 'working in partnership' does not mean that it really is, and some radical critics of social work (such as Margolin, 1997) go as far as to suggest that social work's ostensible purpose of helping and empowering people, is really just cover for its real function which is to manage and control.

All this means that if you are to practise in an ethical way, you need to be able to engage with the politics behind the policies and procedures you are asked to implement. *This* means that you will sometimes be faced with ethical dilemmas, for you may find you disagree in principle with what is expected of you by your employers and by the state. You may even find yourself in a position where you are being asked to do something which you feel strongly will be harmful to your own service users.

A social work student recently discussed with Chris Beckett, for instance, whether it was consistent with the values of social work to take part in 'age assessments' of young asylum seekers, something that she was expected to be involved in as part of her placement. Age assessments are routinely carried out by local authority social workers when asylum seekers who claim to be children look as if they might be older, and local authorities are required to inform the immigration authorities of their conclusions. These assessments have huge implications for the asylum seekers' ability to access services, and even for their ability to stay in the UK. Yet one study found that 'social work managers in some local authority areas instruct, or put pressure on, staff to decide that age disputed individuals [are] over 18 years of age when social workers have assessed them as children' (Crawley, 2007: 78).

There are many different views on immigration. Many, including all the major UK political parties, would argue that control of immigration is necessary for a variety of reasons, including maintaining community cohesion and stability. Others take the view that immigration controls are inherently oppressive and racist (see, for example, Cohen, 2005; Humphries, 2004). If you believe the latter to be the case, then you will presumably take the view that it is unacceptable for a social worker to play any part at all in such a system. Others, though, might argue that the age assessment is really no different in principle from the many other kinds of assessment carried out by social workers that are intended to ensure that limited resources are targeted on those for whom they are intended and/or on those who are most in need of them. ('It isn't racist at all', they might say, 'to try and ensure that services intended for children, are actually delivered to children rather than adults'.) Even if you accept this argument, the question remains: is it appropriate for a social worker to routinely inform the immigration service of the outcome of these assessments?

Kenneth McLaughlin observes that supporting asylum seekers is an entirely appropriate social work role, given social work's special area of responsibility is 'working with those at the margins of society, the disadvantaged and the oppressed, and given that immigrants and asylum seekers are among the most disadvantaged groups in society' (2008: 54), but he points out that this 'support' is seriously compromised if social work agencies are also simultaneously acting, in effect, as an arm of the immigration services. (Age assessments are only one part of this. Social work agencies are required also to report to the Home Office anyone claiming services who they suspect is in the country illegally [McLaughlin, 2008: 55].) What kind of relationship of trust can social workers develop under such circumstances with asylum seekers? Can you really be a genuine supporter of individual migrants in need, and yet also a border guard? If you had a different job, these might be purely theoretical questions that you could discuss with your friends in the pub, but if you are a social worker, they are real choices with which you may be confronted in your day-to-day work. Can I go along with this without selling out my own principles? Can I bring myself to oppose this if it means risking my job?

ASSESSING LAURENT'S AGE

You are working with an asylum seeker from the Democratic Republic of Congo called Laurent. He has arrived in your area having travelled to the UK by lorry. He says he is 16-years-old, and is seeking support from your agency as a child in need. You have no doubt that he came to this country to escape persecution. He bears physical evidence of having been tortured, and you therefore find it convincing when he says that several of his family members have actually been killed by political opponents. You have no doubt that he is frightened of going back to the DRC, and you can also see that he is badly in need of support in the UK, support which your agency will not give him if it is decided that he is an adult. Your agency will also be obliged to report the findings of your age assessment to the immigration authorities (see Children's Legal Centre, 2006).

But Laurent does not look 16 to you. If you saw him in the street, you would guess that he was at least 20. You have been asked by your manager to carry out an age assessment, according to government guidelines. Your manager reminds you that her budget is already stretched to the point that it is already impossible to provide adequate services to care leavers and other young people in the area. How do you respond?

COMMENTS ON EXERCISE 4.2

We suspect that there will be a wide range of views in response to this, but we suggest that simply 'doing what you are told' is not a sufficient response. Social workers *do* have responsibilities towards their employers and to the elected bodies to which their employers are accountable, and cannot expect to always be able to act on the basis of their own personal convictions, but simply 'obeying orders' cannot in all circumstances be an excuse (for, after all, even those who carried out the Nazi holocaust were obeying orders). Human beings, as moral agents, must answer to their own consciences, as well as to their employers and political masters.

We do not wish to suggest that it is acceptable for social workers to simply ignore or flout the rules and expectations placed upon them by their employers and by society, for if public employees were able to simply set aside these rules and expectations and do whatever they thought fit, it would open the way to all kinds of abuses. We should not forget that many have suffered and died in the UK over the centuries (as in other countries) for a state which is answerable to the elected representatives of the people. However, it cannot be the case that a responsible social worker follows rules no matter what. There is necessarily a tension for ethical practitioners between their duties as employees and public servants, and their obligation to act in a way that is consistent with their own understanding as to what is right.

The following example, taken from a book about ethical practice in social work around the world, describes a situation in Denmark, where staff at a primary school took a decision not to report child abuse to the social care authorities but to deal with it in their own way:

> Maryam E. was the class teacher for children in the second grade (8-year-olds) in a state school ... In her class she has 24 children of which around 75% have an immigrant or refugee background. After some incidents of bullying and fights among the children, Maryam E. decided to address the theme of violence and conflict management with the class ... She asked the children to write a letter to her (using words or pictures) about what kind of conflicts they experienced and how they handled them at home. When Maryam E. saw the letters she was 'shocked'. A majority of the letters (70%) were about violence, about the children being hit ... [One] child had drawn a picture of a coat hanger with which he was hit; and another one, a stick. Some children wrote that their mother was hit.
>
> Maryam E. was painfully aware of her legal obligation as a teacher to report to the social authorities about child abuse, but she did not believe it to be the best way to reach the parents and to change the ways in the families. She discussed the problem with the principal of the school and it was decided to confront the parents of the children in the class as a group in order to establish a dialogue about conflict management in the families. No reports were written to the social authorities. What happened was that the school ... invited the parents to a meeting about how to stop violent conflicts in the class. Almost all parents showed up. Through role plays and group discussions the teachers wanted to establish a dialogue with the parents and to make the point that children learn from their parents how to handle conflict ... During the meeting the teachers also told the parents about the letters, and about Danish law. Furthermore, they informed the parents about the teachers' duty to report about violence against children. From the dialogue with the parents the school learned that many immigrant and refugee families in that area live in a 'parallel society' and know very little about the Danish society and Danish norms about bringing up children. (Anonymous case example from Banks and Nøhr, 2011: 179–80)

The decision taken by school staff resulted in the school being heavily criticised in Danish society, first for not fulfilling its legal obligations to report abuse, and second for allegedly applying a double standard and treating immigrant families differently from other Danish families. In the view of the teacher and the school principal, however, the meeting was a success, because there was less violence among the children in the classroom afterwards, and the parents became more willing to open up to school staff about issues at home. As the principal put it:

> If we had sent off a whole pile of reports, then five or six families would probably have turned their backs on us, moved their children to a private school run by their own minority ethnic group and continued to beat their children. Many other parents would have thought that those teachers are not to be trusted, and we shall never again tell them about our family life. (Anon, cited in Banks and Nøhr, 2011: 182)

There is a fine balance to be struck between behaving like an irresponsible maverick, on the one hand, and, on the other, simply following rules in a bureaucratic way. We cannot offer a simple formula here for determining where that line should be drawn, but we do suggest that it is something that a professional social worker needs to grapple with.

Here is another example:

DISCHARGING RUBY FROM HOSPITAL

Ruby White, aged 91, is in hospital following a bad fall in her home in which she broke several bones in her right leg, necessitating surgery. Ruby was very badly shaken by the experience itself and also by the operation. She is anxious, tearful and slightly muddled as a result. She has lost all her confidence. She is very frightened by the prospect of returning home, even with the promise of a high level of domiciliary care, and would very much like a few days longer in hospital to recuperate a bit more, physically and emotionally, before she goes.

As the social worker for Mrs White, you can see that it is very much in her interest for her to be allowed this breathing space. You believe that a precipitate return home could have a serious impact on Mrs White's mental health and her capacity to cope in the long run. However, your agency is under tremendous pressure to move patients out of hospital wards where they are 'blocking beds' and, indeed, your agency is charged a substantial sum of money by the hospital for every day that such patients stay on in hospital. Your manager instructs you to make arrangements for Ruby to return home tomorrow morning. He is simply not interested in discussions about the impact on Ruby's well-being. He says your responsibility is simply to arrange a package of domiciliary care to start tomorrow morning.

How do you respond?

EXERCISE 4.3

COMMENTS ON EXERCISE 4.3

The reason for the pressure to move Ruby White is, of course, to do with limited resources: the health service needs to vacate beds in order to have capacity for new

(Cont'd)

patients needing to come in. It has to be acknowledged, therefore, that a decision to keep Ruby in hospital for longer might be in her own interests but might create more problems for some other elderly person – unknown to you – who needs to come into hospital. Your manager is not insisting you do this out of malice!

There must, however, be for all of us a point at which a system seems so inadequate that we no longer feel able in conscience to lend it legitimacy. We are not saying that this necessarily applies to the above case example. Many social workers are implementing just such a system and we are not suggesting that they are acting unethically in doing so (presumably they would argue that, given the resource constraints, a service like this is the best way of being fair to everyone). A point may come though for any conscientious social worker when she is asked to do something which simply seems wrong and which she is simply not prepared in conscience to do. Suppose, for instance, that, in your judgement, the effect on Ruby of a premature return home could be fatal or irreversible: in such circumstances, you might feel that your professional responsibility for her well-being was simply not compatible with going along with your manager's instructions.

You might try various means to get the decision reversed. For instance, you might ask that the matter be referred to a more senior manager. You might advise Ruby and her family about ways in which they could appeal the decision. But, ultimately, given that you are not actually in a position to act against your agency's own policies, you might be placed in a position where you either had to do something which you felt to be unethical, or had to resign. Your decision would depend on how strongly you felt about the ethical principle at stake.

DEALING WITH POLITICS

Exercises 4.2 and 4.3 illustrated that social workers sometimes find themselves in a position where they are asked to implement policies that they feel will cause real harm to the service users they are supposed to be helping. The example from Denmark illustrated that professionals may sometimes come to this conclusion, even about procedures and practices intended to be helpful. In this case, procedures supposed to protect children would, in the view of the Danish teachers, actually increase the risk to the children. You too are likely in your career in social work to encounter procedures and practices which seem to you unhelpful or counter-productive. This is in part because policies and procedures are the product of a political process, and will reflect many different agendas. The following exercise may help to illustrate what we mean by this.

HIDDEN AGENDAS

Suppose the government produces a new guidance document on the mental health services, which will have implications for social work in this area. The document states that its aims are:

(a) to improve the lives of people who have mental health problems;
(b) to help the carers of people who have mental health problems;
(c) to ensure that members of the public are adequately protected from the small minority of people who have mental health problems who are violent and may pose some risk to others.

What other, unstated, agendas might also lie behind the document?

COMMENTS ON EXERCISE 4.4

Typically, a policy document of any kind will result from a process of negotiation between various interest groups, each with its own agenda. Agendas you may have thought of might include:

- the treasury agenda (pressure to save money);
- the agendas of various interest groups on whom the government relies for political support;
- the need of elected politicians to be seen to be responding to public concerns;
- the agendas of professional associations concerned for the status and well-being of their own members;
- the commercial interests of particular industries (such as the pharmaceutical industry, or companies providing residential care);
- pressure from the media, who have an incentive to dramatise and simplify issues in order to sell papers or attract viewers.

A new policy, ostensibly intended to help a given service user group, will seldom, if ever, serve *only* that purpose and will almost inevitably include aspects which serve other purposes. These other purposes may or may not be consistent with the primary or ostensible aim of the policy. The following are all major factors in the development of the policies under which publicly funded social work operates:

'SOMETHING MUST BE DONE'

If a tragic and well-publicised incident occurs – someone is assaulted by a person with a mental illness, a child is killed as a result of abuse which was not prevented by the child protection service – there is public pressure on politicians for 'something to be done' to stop such incidents recurring. Politicians may be keen to demonstrate that yes, something is indeed being done, but the 'something' they come up with may not necessarily be well thought through or implementable. It may even result in a *worse* service.

The report by Eileen Munro (2011) into the child protection system in England and Wales, proposed to strip out excessive bureaucracy and rigidity in the system, such as prescribed timescales for assessments, on the basis that they 'distort practice' by making professionals worry more about meeting targets than about doing the best for children. This makes a lot of sense, but as Munro herself observes, every one of these cumbersome aspects of the system was introduced in the first place as an attempt to 'do something' about perceived problems in the system. In many cases, they have been put in place following well-publicised child abuse tragedies, when immense pressure is placed on politicians by the media to take some sort of action to prevent similar events occurring again.

COST CUTTING

It is difficult for politicians to admit to cutting back services. Therefore cost-cutting exercises may be presented instead as exciting and innovative approaches to practice. The community care reforms of the 1990s, for instance, were presented to practitioners and the public as a new 'needs-led' approach, but they were driven in large measure by 'the need to stop the haemorrhage in the social security budget, and to do so in a way that would minimise political outcry and not give additional resources to local authorities themselves' (Lewis and Glennerster, 1996).

PLACATING INTEREST GROUPS

In developing new policies, politicians and civil servants will attempt to accommodate the wishes of lobbies and pressure groups that they perceive as being powerful. These will include campaigning organisations and commercial interests. (The burgeoning residential care industry was an important player, for instance, when the community care reforms of the 1990s were being thrashed out.)

Policy documents will typically include concessions which have been made to a number of different groups. These concessions may be very substantial but they may also be little more than 'window-dressing' (what Cobb and Ross [1997: 34] call 'symbolic placation'), gestures to make these groups feel they have achieved something.

As noted above, we need to be aware that our own profession is one of these interest groups. We are ourselves political players, and we should never arrogantly assume that it is only *other* people who have self-serving agendas, while our own motives alone are pure. We too are concerned about our pay, our working conditions, our job security, our status in society, and these concerns necessarily contribute to how we see the world. Kenneth McLaughlin describes an experience of setting up a service for mental health service users, which in fact was little used. 'What struck me,' he observes of the discussions among his colleagues on the steering committee about the low take-up of the service, 'is that not once did anyone consider it possible that perhaps they were not needed' (2008: vi). He goes on:

> Two things were noticeable. First, this echoed with Dineen's ... point that the mental health industry was like any other. To survive, it had to expand, find new markets (by discovering hitherto hidden illnesses or syndromes) and present itself as a solution to these problems. Second, the underlying assumption of the steering committee seemed to be that the public could not cope without their professional input. The possibility that perhaps the majority of the public could manage quite adequately without them was simply not considered. (McLaughlin, 2008: vi, referring to Dineen, 1999)

Each interest group has its own agenda, which is only partly to do with the best interests of service users, and this will be true of our own agendas also.

THE MEDIA

An emotive 'good story' often carries more weight in the media than a complex and difficult argument. Media coverage of dramatic incidents where mentally ill people have committed violent crimes may result in a public perception that these incidents are much more common than they really are, and in pressure to 'do something' to stop them. This in turn may result in politicians and civil servants shaping policy around these concerns rather than around other, less newsworthy but perhaps more important, needs.

In the case of child protection, the media highlight incidents where professional agencies fail to provide protection and a child has died. These are relatively rare and extreme incidents, and little media coverage is given to the day-to-day work of child protection agencies who deal with thousands of cases every day. Nevertheless, the high profile given to these cases means that they have a disproportionately powerful influence on the policy agenda. To make things more complicated, the media also sometimes run stories alleging that social workers are needlessly interfering in family life, or breaking up loving families (see, for instance, *Daily Mail*, 2005). Child protection policy in the UK can be observed to be swinging first one way and then the other, as it attempts to respond to these contradictory demands for 'something to be done'.

Policy formation, then, is influenced by many forces other than a purely rational and altruistic consideration of the best interests of service users. The ethical implications of this are considerable, for it raises the possibility that the interests of service users may sometimes be sacrificed in favour of other, competing interests (such as making politicians look good, or keeping the social services department off the front page of the newspapers), and it is difficult to see how an ethical practitioner can collude in this. In the next chapter, we will discuss what we will call a 'duty of realism'. Part of that duty, it seems to us, lies in refusing to collude with gestures which are presented as being helpful to service users but in fact are not. (We should note, incidentally, that while the discussion has centred so far on state-funded organisations, voluntary organisations are certainly not exempt from the kinds of competing political pressures that we have been discussing. Even agencies with no state funding have their own sets of competing stakeholders to consider [see Hudson, 1995].)

SOCIAL WORK, RADICALISM AND SOCIAL CHANGE

> ## Radical
>
> The word 'radical' refers to 'getting to the root of things', and radicals in politics, whether of the left or the right, are those who seek to bring about 'root and branch' change rather than simply tinkering with details. The two most radical governments in the recent history of the UK were arguably the post-war Labour government of Clement Attlee, which set up the welfare state, and the Conservative government of Margaret Thatcher, elected in 1979, which broke the post-war consensus on the welfare state, and took the country in a new neoliberal direction which both major parties have since followed, in which private enterprise and the market economy were given a much wider role, and publicly owned services are viewed as problematic and constantly in need of reform on more market-orientated lines.

Up to now, we have been mainly discussing ethical issues arising from the fact that social workers are faced with, and expected to implement, political decisions made by others. But social workers' political obligations are widely regarded within the profession as extending much further than that, extending to a requirement to actively promote political change. Thus, for instance, the National Association of Social Workers in the USA states that 'Social workers promote social justice and social change with and on behalf of clients' (NASW, 2008), and the International Federation of Social Workers offers a definition of social work which puts social justice and social change at centre stage (IFSW, 2004).

Why should social workers concern themselves with these wider political issues? We will answer this by means of an analogy.

EXERCISE 4.5

THE COMPANY DOCTOR AND THE TOXIC CHEMICALS

Suppose a company doctor, working in a chemical factory, begins to wonder why she is so regularly treating patients with bronchitis. When she looks further into it, she discovers that the bronchitis is associated with exposure to a particular chemical used in the manufacturing process in the factory, owned by the very company that employs her on a good salary. What are the doctor's options, and what *should* she do?

COMMENTS ON EXERCISE 4.5

The doctor *could*, if she wanted, decide that her job was to simply treat the patients with bronchitis, however the illness was caused. She could decide that company policy was none of her business. But is this an ethical position? If she did this, would she not be effectively covering up the true cause of the problem, by making the bronchitis look as if it was simply an individual problem of the patients? If the doctor is genuinely interested in the health of her patients, does she not have an obligation to draw attention to the fact that the factory's practices are causing health problems? Should she not pressure the company to protect its staff from the harmful chemical? Should she not inform the workers themselves and perhaps work alongside them to bring about change? And is this not the case, even if it would put her job and her salary at risk?

A radical critique from the political left of traditional casework-based social work has long been that it makes the structural problems of society look like 'individual inadequacies' (Bailey and Brake, 1975: 147). From this perspective, a social worker who simply does casework with her clients and does not concern herself with wider social questions, is a bit like the doctor in Exercise 4.5. Just as the bronchitis the doctor was treating was not just a random illness which some of her patients happened to get, but a consequence of the factory's practices, so the various problems with which social workers deal are not simply the result of individual inadequacies, but a result of the way society is organised.

If you are born and grow up in a run-down housing estate, where there is 50% unemployment, poor housing stock, failing educational facilities, a high crime rate, a high rate of teenage pregnancies, widespread use of illegal drugs, general malnutrition and a culture of low expectation, then this is not your personal fault. It is the result of living in a particular kind of society which tolerates unemployment, poor housing and poor facilities for some, while allowing others to accumulate vast wealth. And if, in these circumstances, you get involved in crime, or find it hard to be a good parent, or get involved in substance abuse, this too is not simply your fault. Yes, you are still responsible for your choices, but the menu of options you have to choose from is vastly different from the menu available, say, to the son of an insurance executive and a PR consultant, who grows up in a leafy suburb, attends private schools and Oxford University, and then gets a well-paid job in the City of London by making use of the contacts of his parents and the parents of his friends.

All this is not to say that it is necessarily helpful for you to think of yourself as a 'victim' (a point often made from the political *right*), nor that it would necessarily be *un*helpful to you to receive a service in the form of individual casework, just as it is not unhelpful of the doctor in our example to treat her patients' bronchitis. (Obviously, however they contracted the disease, it does still need treating.) But casework in itself will not solve the wider problem, and more insidiously, it may serve to conceal the wider problem, by making it look as if everything necessary is being done. So, while it may well be that a social worker is genuinely helping her individual clients if she simply does casework with them and does not worry about the bigger picture, is she not colluding in a kind of cover-up by doing so, a kind of dishonesty, just as the doctor would be colluding in a cover-up if she simply treated the bronchitis while doing nothing about its causes?

This line of argument takes us to a radical view of the moral obligations of a social worker that goes far beyond the traditional professional ethical obligations to exercise fairness and impartiality in dealing with service users. Iain Ferguson and Rona Woodward point out that, in the past, this radical view was more common, sometimes to the point that there was no clear dividing line between social work, community work and political activism: 'Individuals like Emmeline Pethick-Lawrence, Sylvia Pankhurst and George Lansbury made little distinction between their political activities as socialists and suffragists and their efforts to provide direct support to the poor' (2009: 21, 153ff.).

The extent to which political activism can, or should, be combined with day-to-day social work practice depends on context, and is also a matter of debate. Kenneth McLaughlin (2008) argues that blurring the line between the personal and political arenas may actually work *against* the interests of service users. Anne Wilson and Peter Beresford question the 'grandiose' statements about social work's capacity to transform society that are found in some social work texts. 'We find such statements surprising,' they observe, 'given social work's low status and overt social control functions' (2000: 558). And Karen Healy warns against 'delusions of grandeur that all too readily become nightmares for many subjects of social welfare systems' (2008: 195). These are important and valid concerns, shared by the present authors, but they do not in fact undermine the core of the radical argument, which is, as we have seen, that to treat symptoms without addressing the underlying problem is to collude in a kind of cover-up. As Ferguson and Woodward observe, 'the profession cannot claim to seek social justice if all it does is to focus on individual needs and behaviour' (2009: 162). If social workers are not politically engaged, they run the risk of being part of the problem rather than part of the solution.

We will not attempt to generalise about the form that political engagement should take, not least because (as Exercise 4.1 would have illustrated), different readers of this book will have different political understandings and political priorities, but the kinds of political engagement advocated by Ferguson and Woodward range from what they call '"guerrilla warfare" and small-scale resistance' within the workplace to 'collective activity and political campaigning' outside it (2009: 153).

The phrase 'guerrilla warfare' is borrowed by these authors from a state-employed social worker participating in a focus group, who described how he and his colleagues had decided to simply ignore requirements to produce elaborate time-consuming documentation which, in their view, served no purpose other than to capture management information required for performance indicators. Instead, they continued to work 'in a way that's friendly to service users and useful to staff' (2009: 158). Another participant in the same focus group, also a state-employed social worker, was 'unwilling to turn a blind eye to unmet need and service user distress' and described how she 'almost constantly "passed information back up the line to senior managers"' (2009: 158).

Collective activity and political campaigning are options available to any social worker acting outside of their day-to-day work context, whether acting in a private capacity, or acting in concert with colleagues. Which campaigns, and which collective activities, are of course a matter for individuals to decide on, on the basis of the injustices they witness in the workplace, and what they understand to be the root causes of those injustices, but we do not think that anyone who implements the policies of the state and/or works with people on the margins of society, can honestly say that 'politics has nothing to do with me'.

The BASW Code of Ethics states: 'Social workers, individually, collectively and with others have a duty to challenge social conditions that contribute to social exclusion, stigmatisation or subjugation, and work towards an inclusive society' (2012: 9). This surely must be so. How could we claim to be genuinely acting in the interests of service users, or supporting them in resolving problems, if we take no interest in the conditions that bring about those problems in the first place?

CHAPTER SUMMARY

In this chapter, we have encouraged you to think of political questions as being very much a part of what you need to think about when considering ethical practice in social work. We have shown that social work itself is very much a political creation, and pointed out that the policies and practices that social workers implement are the products of a political process. We have argued that the political process itself involves many stakeholders and may be driven by other considerations than simply the best interests of your service users, which can place you in a position where your obligations to your service users may be at odds with the expectations that your employers have of you. We discussed the profession's often-stated commitment to social justice and social change, arguing that an ethical social work practitioner cannot simply ignore the structural injustices that lie behind the individual problems of service users, and we have considered different views about the ways in which social workers should engage with this wider political agenda. We concluded that, while there are different views on what form this engagement should take, no social worker can truthfully claim that politics is not of his or her concern.

 FURTHER READING

The following, which we have quoted here, is a recent call for a more politically radical approach to social work:

Ferguson, I. and Woodward, R. (2009) *Radical Social Work in Practice: Making a Difference*. Bristol: Policy Press.

The following book, referred to several times in this chapter, provides an interesting and original take on the subject; it is politically committed, but critical of the 'radical' approach as it is commonly formulated:

McLaughlin, K. (2008) *Social Work, Politics and Society*. Bristol: Policy Press.

Those wishing to challenge their own assumptions about the role of social work in society may like to read:

Margolin, L. (1997) *Under the Cover of Kindness: The Invention of Social Work*. Charlottesville, VA: University of Virginia Press.

5

REALISM AS AN ETHICAL PRINCIPLE

- About realism
- Realism about practice decisions
- Realism and language
- Realism at the core of ethical thinking

In the first edition of this book, we proposed an ethical principle for social work that we called 'the duty of realism'. Chris Beckett has developed this idea since (2006, 2007, 2009) and other texts have taken it up, so it seemed appropriate, in this edition, to give it a chapter to itself.

Put simply, what we mean by the 'duty of realism' is that responsible social workers should take due account of *how things actually are*. We don't claim great originality for this idea, but we think there is value in foregrounding the principle and making it explicit. As we discussed in the previous chapter, social work is a product of politics. Social work discourse, like all political discourses, is a confusing mix of the substantive and the purely rhetorical, in which words can be used misleadingly, and claims can be made which would be hard to support in fact. Hugely ambitious goals are set for social work by its political masters. Even more ambitious goals are sometimes set by social work academics and by practising social workers themselves. And, because social work is not an 'exact science' – we frequently have no way of measuring the effects of our own actions with any degree of precision, or even at all – we may easily deceive ourselves that to set out these grand objectives is the same thing as achieving them.

Service users, however, must live with the actual consequences of our actions – not with our good intentions nor with our dreams – so it is important to try and make distinctions between the imaginary and the real. Kerstin Svensson observes that we need to 'be careful to avoid making the assumption that social work is necessarily a way of *being* good, as if this were irrespective of what social workers actually *do*' (2009: 247).

ABOUT REALISM

Realism

1 'the attitude or practice of accepting a situation as it is and being prepared to deal with it accordingly...'.

2 'the quality or fact of representing a person or thing in a way that is accurate and true to life ...'. (*Oxford Dictionary of English*, 2009)

The word 'realism' is used in a number of different ways. It has a specific meaning in philosophy, for instance, and another meaning in political science. However, we use the word here pretty much as it is used in everyday speech, to mean taking due account of the realities of the situation under discussion. Of course, this immediately begs the question as to what we mean by 'realities'. Social constructionists have taught us to be wary of the naive idea that reality is something fixed and 'out there' as opposed to something fluid, constructed and negotiated.

But naivety in the opposite direction is also possible, and is quite prevalent in contemporary academic social work where, as Bob Pease observes, many 'have moved away from positivism, science and [so he suggests!] rationality' (2009: 195). In fact, there are a lot of aspects of life that we can all agree to be real. Even the most ardent post-modernists and social constructionists avoid walking into brick walls or jumping from high buildings. The aim of this chapter is not to deny that 'reality' is a complex thing, but rather to argue that we should not do the equivalent, in social work practice terms, of walking into walls or jumping from high buildings. (Philosophical debates about realism are outside the scope of this book, but interested readers might like to look at Hammersley's idea of 'subtle realism' [1992] or Bhaskar's 'critical realism' [1989]. Also of relevance is 'left realism', originating in criminology: see, for instance, Currie [2010].)

Our point here is *not* that we must simply accept things the way they are, but that 'the ways things are' is something that we do need to take seriously if we want to change things for the better. To quote Bob Pease again:

Social constructivists and postmodernists have emphasised the importance of seeing science and knowledge as being socially constructed. However ... if there is no objective reality, how can we develop the foundations for emancipatory projects? (2009: 195)

'Realism' and 'radicalism' may seem at first sight to be very different to one another, or even opposites, but actually, properly understood, they are closely related. Both are about getting to the bottom of things.

REALISM ABOUT PRACTICE DECISIONS

WORDS, INTENTIONS AND DEEDS

You are about to have surgery on your heart. You get to meet the doctor who is to perform the operation. She is one of the nicest and kindest people you have ever met. She does everything possible to make you feel listened to and supported. Then she tells you that she has had very little experience of performing any kind of surgery, and none whatsoever of heart surgery. Indeed, she admits she knows very little about the anatomy of the heart. 'But never mind,' she says, 'I promise I will do my very best for you and that's the main thing after all!'

Your friend sincerely believes she is a good listener. She often tells you how good a listener she is. In fact, she spends so much time telling you about it, that you can hardly get a word in yourself.

What is the common strand here? What might be a social work equivalent of behaving in these ways?

Comments on Exercise 5.1

Given the title of the chapter, you will doubtless have spotted that the common strand is a lack of realism. You might be pleased to have a heart surgeon who was a kind person, but you'd certainly want more than just that: heart surgery requires skill and knowledge and not just kindness. (In fact, we would rather put up with a heart surgeon who was mean and unpleasant, as long as she was good at heart surgery.) Your friend might well think she is a good listener, but she really isn't, and just saying she is does not alter that fact.

You may have thought of other social work equivalents but here are ours:

1   There are many interventions which social workers would be ill-advised to engage in, without appropriate training, skills and resources – for example, in-depth thera-peutic interventions with people who have experienced profound abuse.
2   Social work students often write in essays that they worked 'in partnership' with service users, but just saying that work has been done in partnership doesn't make it

(Cont'd)

true. For a working relationship to be a partnership, both partners need to feel that they have entered into it, voluntarily and on an equal basis, and whether we like it or not, many working relationships in social work are with involuntary service users, who have little choice but to engage with the social worker, since they may face sanctions, or lose services, if they don't. Language is important, and it can change the way we see the world, but one of the features of language is that it can be used to tell untruths. We can't change the nature of a relationship just by giving it a different name, and we can't abolish power differences by talking as if they weren't there.

Working as a social worker, you will often encounter people living in appallingly difficult circumstances: children whose parents treat them badly every day, old people who do without food to pay for fuel, migrants escaping from brutal persecution in their own countries who find themselves treated like criminals in this one. Since you came into social work to make a positive difference, you very naturally and properly want to use your position as a social worker to improve things for the people you work with, and incidentally to make yourself feel like a good and useful person. It is entirely appropriate that you should be motivated in this way, but there are some dangers in it, for in our desire to feel good about ourselves we may over-reach ourselves.

Of course, it is important to set our sights high, to believe in ourselves, and to encourage others to believe in themselves. Many of us are capable in fact of doing much more remarkable things than we believe ourselves to be, but this does not mean we are capable of doing everything. We can illustrate this as follows. Imagine a father who is teaching his daughter to ride a bicycle. He is running along behind her saying 'Go on, you can do it, you can do it!' Sure enough, buoyed up by her father's belief in her, the girl pedals away and pretty soon is riding the bicycle on her own. Now imagine a father who is encouraging his daughter to jump from the top of a high building. 'Go on,' he says, 'fly! You can do it if you make up your mind to it.' Encouragement and self-belief help us to acquire skills such as riding a bicycle because riding a bicycle *is something that most people are actually capable of doing*, but no amount of self-belief or encouragement will enable someone to escape the pull of gravity and fly.

So setting our sights high, and encouraging others to do likewise, is frequently entirely consistent with the duty of realism, because it is an observable fact that people flourish on encouragement, and that people often underestimate their own capabilities. But that is not the same thing as saying that positive thoughts and good intentions will overcome *every* obstacle, whatever we may have been led to believe by countless Hollywood movies.

Indeed, as important as self-belief undoubtedly is, the idea that the *only* thing that holds us back in life is lack of self-belief is politically a rather questionable one, since it implies that, when people are not very successful in life, this reflects their own personal shortcomings, rather than their circumstances. (Hollywood movies tend to promote the 'American Dream' that everything is possible for anyone who tries hard enough: it is a pretty convenient dream for the wealthy and powerful.) In the real world, we, as social workers, have to consider what is practicable in terms of our own skills, in terms of the capabilities of our service users, and in terms of the time and resources that we and our service users have at our disposal. If we don't consider these practical things, we will be setting our service users up to fail, just as the father on top of the tall building would be setting up his daughter to fail if he told her that all she needed was self-belief in order to be able to fly. The wrong intervention, or a poorly delivered intervention, or an intervention which is started but not completed, can sometimes make a bad situation even worse, as illustrated by the enthusiastic but ill-prepared heart surgeon in Exercise 5.1. We would suggest that the following three questions all need to be considered by a responsible social worker, appropriately concerned to protect the interests of service users:

- *Competence.* Do I, and whoever else will be involved in delivering this intervention, possess the necessary skills and expertise to successfully implement it? (This point is made in the BASW Code of Ethics which states that social workers should recognise the limits of their practice [2012: 15].)
- *Resources.* Do I have reasonable grounds to believe that the necessary resources will be available to see this intervention through? It may feel heroic to say 'Never mind the resources, this needs to be done, so I'm going to do it', but social work should not be about making yourself feel like a hero, it should be about doing the best you can by your clients. We are not arguing here that social workers should simply accept resource limitations – it may be appropriate to demand more – but to pretend you can act without taking resources into account is dishonest and dangerous, and, what is more, it plays into the hands of those who argue that resources are not a problem. (There will be more on this in Chapter 10.)
- *Evidence about outcomes.* Do I have reasonable grounds to believe that this kind of intervention, with this particular client in this particular situation, is reasonably likely to have a successful outcome, and reasonably unlikely to cause serious harm to my client?

An example of the last point is provided by the case of 'permanent' placement of children who cannot live in their families of origin. It is generally accepted (including by the present writers) that, in such situations, it is important to try, if possible, to provide children with a secure, loving and stable permanent family, whether in an adoptive home, a long-term foster home or with relatives. It is important that children are carefully prepared for these 'permanent' placements, to which they are typically moved after a fairly lengthy period of being exposed to serious problems in their family of origin, followed by another lengthy period in temporary placements while a decision is made about their long-term future.

Social workers sometimes present these 'permanent' placements to children as their 'forever families', but evidence suggests that, the older the child at the time of placement, the more likely it is that these 'permanent' arrangements will in fact break down. For example, Fratter et al. (1991: 115), following up a large sample of adoptions and 'permanent' foster placements made by voluntary agencies, found that for children placed between the ages of 3 and 4, the risk of breakdown had already doubled as against the risk for those placed under 3, while for children placed aged 5–8, the breakdown rate was six times higher than for under 3s, becoming nearly a 1 in 5 chance of breakdown. The rate doubled again for those aged 9–11 at placement, becoming a risk greater than 1 in 3. (For a more recent study drawing similar conclusions about the increasing difficulty of providing real permanence for older children, see also Biehal et al., 2010.)

This is a good example of a situation where good intentions are sometimes confused with good outcomes. It feels very good, when a child's home is abusive or neglectful, to place him with adults willing to welcome him as a permanent member of their family. If the placement fails, however, one or two years later, when the adoptive or foster parents find they are unable to cope with the child anymore and ask for him to be moved, then this is *not* a good outcome. Indeed, it must often be a really devastating experience for children who will have already been moved from their families of origin, and may have been through a number of moves since. And this raises an ethical question. However much we might *like* to secure permanency for older children in public care, at what point does it become unfair and dishonest to place a child with a family and present this placement to the child as the home where he or she will remain for good, and at what point does this amount to setting a child up to fail?

Conversely, and equally importantly, one might also ask how long it is right to carry on struggling to keep a child in their family of origin in situations where the prospects for success are very low, knowing as we do that 'delaying difficult decisions about entry into care, or delaying decisions about permanency, may mean that children lose their chance of adoption or … of stable foster care' (Biehal et al., 2010: 272).

The answers to these questions are not easy, but our point here is that these judgements and decision should be based on an understanding of what outcomes are actually likely (just as surgical procedures or medical treatments should be made on the basis of evidence about what procedures actually work), as well as on a realistic appraisal of the resources available (availability of placements, social work time and access to long-term support). They should not just be based on wishful thinking.

The same kind of test, incidentally, can be applied not only to our own practice decisions, but to whole new policy initiatives. 'Will this actually work and be helpful, given the resources available?' is the question that we should ask when a new initiative is rolled out. 'Or is it essentially a political gesture whose true purpose is simply to demonstrate that "something is being done"?'

REALISM AND LANGUAGE

The previous section was about checking the match between aspirations and reality. We will now move on to the match between reality and *language*. Human beings use language to express, understand and shape the world, but, as we pointed out earlier, language can also be used to mislead. We can use it to mislead others, but, even more insidiously, we can use it to mislead ourselves. For instance, in Exercise 5.1, we mentioned the use of the phrase 'working in partnership' used in a student essay to describe a working relationship with an involuntary service user. We are not suggesting that such a phrase is ever used with a deliberate intention to deceive, but we do suggest that by using the phrase, and thinking of the relationship as a partnership, the student may be concealing from herself its true nature.

In the previous chapter, we referred to Leslie Margolin's view (1997) that social workers' belief that they are in business to help and empower, can easily serve to conceal, not only from others, but from themselves, their (in his view) true purpose of controlling troublesome elements in society. You may think this is *too* bleak a view, and we would agree with you, but he is right to emphasise that what we *tell* ourselves we are doing is not necessarily the same thing as what we are in fact doing. The frequent – one might say almost obsessive – use in social work discourse of language that is emancipatory in tone ('empowerment', 'partnership', 'person-centred', 'anti-oppressive', 'user-led') is, we think, striking, when one remembers that a large proportion of social work service users are in fact involuntary clients, and how much of social work time is spent on exercising control over people using the legal powers and coercive resources of the state.

Changing the name of a thing is a lot easier than changing the substance of it, and repeating a virtuous-sounding word (Beckett, 2009) is easier than actually practising consistently in a virtuous fashion. Words are just sounds, or letters on a page, and have no intrinsic value. Their only value lies in the meaning they convey. If words are overused, or misused, or repeated unthinkingly in a purely ritual way, their meaning quite quickly fades or changes. It makes no sense just to continue repeating the words regardless, without paying attention to 'what the terms mean, and in what way their meaning has changed over time' (McLaughlin, 2008: 51). In fact, if we accord virtue to words in their own right, and use them simply as a way of making ourselves feel or seem virtuous, they can end up becoming a way of concealing reality. Ian Butler and Mark Drakeford are referring to this kind of danger when they speak of 'the flexible exploitation of ambiguity which has allowed social work to retain the semblance of loyalty to its own values, while carrying out the bidding of political masters with very different ideas and purposes' (2001: 8). After all, if social workers accept words like 'empowerment' or 'partnership' as being, of themselves, badges of virtue, then all any government needs to do to secure their co-operation, is to sprinkle policy documents with words of this kind.

We would therefore encourage you to be careful about taking virtuous-sounding buzzwords, such as 'person-centred', 'anti-oppressive', 'personalisation', 'empowerment' or 'partnership', at face value, and to be careful also about your own use of them, ensuring that you only use them when you are clear what you mean by them. As Iain Ferguson observes, the connotations of these sorts of words are 'overwhelmingly positive and they are therefore very hard to be "against", without sounding mean or curmudgeonly. Who, for example, could be *against* empowerment or against "choice" in health and social care services?' (Ferguson, 2007: 388, original emphasis).

They can therefore easily be used as a means of closing down the debate. This is not to deny that these words refer to important principles. On the contrary, our point is that these principles are too important for their names to be used as mere badges of virtuousness.

WORKING WITH LISA: REALISM ABOUT WORKING RELATIONSHIPS

You are working with a young mother, Lisa, whose son James is subject to a child protection plan, as a result of poor care connected with Lisa's heroin use, and her recently ended relationship with a violent man. You are the key worker for James, but feel you have established a good working relationship with Lisa. You like her and she seems to like you. She seems willing to talk to you about very personal aspects of her life. You have listened carefully to her views and perspectives. You have worked hard to make clear to her that you are not there to judge her in a moral or personal sense. You have tried your best to ensure that, as far as possible, you work with her on problems that she herself identifies as difficulties in her life, though there are certain basic requirements that she has agreed to adhere to as part of the child protection plan.

What would be a realistic way of describing the kind of working relationship you have established?

Comments on Exercise 5.2

This is the kind of working relationship that, in our experience, is quite often described as 'working in partnership'. In some respects, it does indeed resemble a partnership, in that you are trying to agree an agenda with Lisa rather than impose one on her. However, the bottom line here is that you, not Lisa, are the one in the position of power. You are the one who would have to report back to the child protection conference in the event that Lisa did not adhere to the requirements in the plan. You are the one that might end up taking James' case to court if the situation were to deteriorate to a point where he was at risk of serious harm. It is fine to describe the way you are trying to work as respectful or non-judgemental, but to describe it as a partnership is to draw a veil over power difference. As we have already mentioned, and will discuss further in Chapter 7, social workers are rather prone to emphasise the caring and supportive side of their role and minimise the controlling side, but an honest description of this relationship would need to include both parts of your role.

REALISM AT THE CORE OF ETHICAL THINKING

One of us (Beckett, 2007) has previously borrowed Freud's term 'The Reality Principle' to provide a title for an article about 'the duty of realism'. In fact, Freud wasn't talking about an *ethical* principle when he used the phrase. He was referring to the basis on which the mature human ego supposedly acts in its dealings with the world, as opposed to the infantile 'pleasure principle' which is what drives the id. According to Freud:

> The ego represents what may be called reason and common sense, in contrast to the id, which contains the passions ... in its relation to the id it is like a man on horseback, who has to hold in check the superior strength of the horse. (Freud, 1923: 25)

Experience suggests that in human discourse there is an equivalent dynamic which tends to pull us away from using language and thinking as a way of trying to represent reality, and towards using language and thinking to generate comforting belief systems to make us feel good about ourselves and make ourselves the heroes of the story: a discourse, one might say, that is shaped by the pleasure principle rather than by the reality principle. But this is essentially infantile behaviour. Our point in this chapter has been that mature and responsible human beings need to resist this impulse, and recognise that how the world is, and how we would like it to be, are two different things. We do not have to *accept* the world as it is, but if we want to make things better in the future, in the real world and not just in daydreams, the world as it is must be our starting point.

Straying into an area which more properly belongs to philosophers than to social work educators, we will offer, as a final, tentative thought, the idea that perhaps, at bottom, the basis for *all* ethics is realism. As discussed in Chapter 1, the philosopher David Hume famously argued that you could not derive an 'ought' from an 'is', and certainly it is true that in any given situation, the mere facts will not tell us what we ought to do, however much we might sometimes wish that they would. Yet, in a more general sense, perhaps an understanding of the way things really are is *precisely* what should form the basis for how we ought to behave. It is generally agreed, for instance, that it is wrong, in a moral sense, for a person to behave as if he were the centre of the universe. Is this not so because, as *a matter of fact*, no one *is* the centre of the universe? It seems to us that we have pretty much come back here to Kant's categorical imperative (as discussed in Chapter 2), which says that human beings should not be treated as means but as ends, and that no one should perform in a way which he would not wish others to act in too. Why are these things wrong? They are wrong because, as a matter of fact, none of us *is* a special case. An idea of the world with you as the centre of everything is simply not realistic.

What we have done in this chapter, we suggest, is to try and explore the implications of this general principle of *respecting the way things actually are*.

CHAPTER SUMMARY

In this chapter, we have proposed that being realistic is itself an important ethical principle in social work. While acknowledging that 'reality' is itself a complex idea, we suggested that, nevertheless, a responsible social worker must try to apply a 'reality check' to her own ideas and practice, as well as to the policy framework within which she is intended to work. We need to try to set aside our own wishes and needs, when considering a course of action, and ask ourselves what the outcome for the service user is likely to be.

We also discussed the relationship between language and reality, noting that language can have the effect of deceiving or concealing things. We concluded with some more general thoughts about the relationship between realism and ethics.

 FURTHER READING

We do not know of other books that cover precisely the same ground as this chapter. The following, however, are two comparatively recent texts that have cited 'the duty of realism', as described in the first edition of this book:

Clifford, D. and Burke, B. (2008) *Anti-oppressive Ethics and Values in Social Work*. Basingstoke: Palgrave.

Tanner, D. and Harris, J. (2008) *Working with Older People*. London: Routledge.

PART 2

VALUES AND ETHICS
IN PRACTICE

6

BEING PROFESSIONAL

- Values at work
- Professionalism
- Professional ethics
- Real-world challenges
- Limitations of cases and codes

In Part 1 of this book, we looked at various strands and dimensions to thinking about values and ethics, in each case considering their relevance to social work. We discussed philosophical approaches to ethical questions; we acknowledged and explored the degree to which religion still plays a part in many people's thinking about questions of right and wrong; we noted that issues of values and ethics are not confined to our personal dealings with other people, but are also inseparable from politics; and finally we discussed the relationship between 'reality' (complicated as that is) and ethics, arguing that to practise ethically, it is important to check on the real-world context and outcomes of what you do, and to check that the language you use is congruent with what you are actually doing.

The chapters in this second part of the book are focused more closely on specific challenges that arise in social work practice. We begin by looking at what it means to be professional.

VALUES AT WORK

As we observed in Chapter 1, our values, and the values of the society around us, inform the choices we make, not just at work but in every area of life. But there are several important ways in which a working context is different from other contexts in which we act and make choices. The rules of conduct which we apply in everyday life are not necessarily sufficient to cover our conduct at work for reasons which include the following:

- Some pieces of behaviour which might be perfectly acceptable in a non-work context may not be acceptable in a work context. It is not regarded as acceptable, for instance, for a professional such as a social worker, doctor or teacher to enter into a sexual or romantic relationship with a service user, patient or pupil, even if both parties are adults.
- Conversely, in a professional role, we may need to behave in ways that fall outside what would be acceptable in everyday life. Surgeons cut people open; lawyers present arguments on behalf of their clients which they do not necessarily personally agree with; social workers, acting as Approved Mental Health Professionals under the 2007 and 1983 Mental Health Acts, make decisions which can result in people being detained against their will, something that would be a criminal act in private life.
- When we are at work, we are not just there to be ourselves, we are there to perform a certain role for the benefit of others (whether they are called patients, customers, clients, pupils, students or service users), who need to know what to expect from us in terms of what we can offer and in terms of standards of conduct (see Exercise 6.1 below).
- When we are at work, we are there to perform certain functions on behalf of our employers and/or our clients. We are not there just to do as we think fit, but to fulfil our contract with our employers or clients.

In a working context, it is necessary, for all these reasons, to have certain agreed standards of behaviour. Some of these may be specific to a particular employment contract, but others will be more general and take the form of standards which are supposed to apply across a whole profession. Written codes of professional ethics (BASW, 2012; GSCC, 2010, and their equivalents in other countries, such as NASW, 2008, in the USA) are attempts to capture these standards in writing.

Before going on, you might like to consider this from the perspective of a user of services.

EXERCISE 6.1

YOU AND YOUR DOCTOR

When you visit your doctor, what expectations would you have of him or her in terms of standards of conduct? How do these expectations differ from those that you would have of a friend?

Comments on Exercise 6.1

Here are some that occur to us:

- You would expect your doctor not to pass on information to others without your express permission. With a friend, you would probably work on the assumption that it was all right to pass on your news unless you made it clear that you did not want this to happen.

- You would expect doctors to keep themselves up to date on the health problems which you come to see them about, and to possess and maintain a certain level of skill and knowledge about the recognition and treatment of illnesses.
- You would expect your doctor – even if of the opposite sex – to be able, if necessary, to examine intimate parts of your body without making you feel that the encounter was in any way a sexual one, or one that would alter the nature of your relationship with the doctor.
- You would expect your doctor to provide you with a service regardless of his or her personal feelings about you as a person.
- You would not expect the above standards of behaviour to require individual negotiation. So, for instance, in the event that you had to see another doctor in the absence of your own, you would expect the same standards to be adhered to.

To come at the same question in another way, the following exercise offers some examples of situations in which (we think) a social worker inappropriately crosses the boundary of her professional role:

QUESTIONABLE BEHAVIOUR BY SOCIAL WORKERS

EXERCISE 6.2

If you agree with us that the social workers in the following examples have behaved inappropriately, how would you describe the social worker's mistake in each case?

- The social worker for a 10-year-old boy, David, has established a very good working relationship with him. When she leaves her job to take up a new post elsewhere, she promises always to keep in touch with him.
- A social worker informs a disabled man, Arthur, that she has not been able to obtain for him a service that he had requested and which she had agreed was appropriate to his needs. 'If I was in charge you would get it, Arthur,' she says, 'but unfortunately my managers only seem to think about money'.
- A 15-year-old girl, Lisa, hints that she has been sexually abused. Her social worker encourages her to talk, telling her that 'It's safe to tell me anything you want. I'm just here to listen to whatever you want to say'.
- A social worker, acting as an Approved Mental Health Professional under the 2007 Mental Health Act, signs an application for a woman called Judy to be detained in a mental hospital under Section 2 of the 1983 Mental Health Act. The social worker doesn't think the legal grounds have been strictly met (Judy has been diagnosed as suffering from a mental illness, but there isn't really any evidence that Judy poses a serious risk to herself or others), but the social worker decides to sign anyway because she believes that admission to hospital for assessment would be in Judy's best interests.

Comments on Exercise 6.2

- It is extremely important not to make promises you can't keep to children, particularly to children who already have reason not to trust the adult world. Will this social worker really be arranging her life in ten years' time so she can keep in touch with David? Will it really be in David's interests to maintain contact with his former social worker when he needs to build a working relationship with his new social worker?
- Arthur will be disappointed and perhaps angered by the decision, and the social worker is trying to avoid being the focus of that anger by blaming her managers, but is it really fair to say her managers are only interested in money? If she was a manager herself, would she not also have to try and keep within the budget? This social worker is attempting to redraw the boundary between the agency and the service user in such a way that she places herself on the side of the service user. Since she is in fact part of the agency, isn't this fundamentally dishonest?
- It actually isn't safe for Lisa to tell the social worker anything – or not safe in the way that Lisa is likely to understand it. In the UK context, if Lisa discloses serious abuse, the social worker will be obliged to activate child protection procedures. This could result in a number of consequences which Lisa might well not want. It might lead to the break-up of Lisa's family, since the alleged abuser is likely to be arrested and could be charged and sent to prison. In some circumstances, it might result in Lisa and other children in the family being taken into care. What happens once she has spoken will be outside Lisa's control and also outside the social worker's control. The social worker is therefore seriously misleading Lisa as to the boundaries within which she is operating.
- Here, the social worker is acting illegally and is overriding another person's rights. She is taking it on herself to set aside the safeguards in the law which set limits to the circumstances under which people can be detained against their will.

PROFESSIONALISM

Bricklaying and plumbing are not generally described as professions (the word 'trade' is more commonly used), but we do speak of bricklayers and plumbers performing a 'professional job' if the work is done well. 'Professionalism' is something to be admired and emulated, while lack of professionalism is to be criticised and avoided. The word 'professional', when used in this way, means 'competent', 'thorough', 'skilful', 'conscientious'.

However, we use the word 'professional', and its opposite 'unprofessional', in a more specific way when we speak of 'unprofessional conduct', or say that 'X acted in a thoroughly professional way in difficult circumstances'. This is because we are not just talking about the quality of the work these individuals produce, but about a certain way of conducting themselves.

WHAT DO WE MEAN BY UNPROFESSIONAL?

Think of instances of behaviour on the part of a social worker – or another professional such as a doctor – which you would regard as unprofessional. What does 'unprofessional' mean? What do we mean by 'acting in a professional way'?

Comments on Exercise 6.3

The sorts of things that you have thought of may have included:

- gossiping about information given in confidence;
- showing favouritism;
- entering into a sexual relationship with a service user or patient;
- basing decisions on whether you liked or disliked a person rather than on their needs;
- using your position to sell something to a service user or patient;
- using your position to pressure or coerce a service user or patient into doing something for you.

Why we regard all these behaviours as unprofessional, we would suggest, is that they all involve the person concerned stepping outside of their assigned professional role in order to meet personal needs or desires of their own, or indulge their own personal preferences.

Behaving 'professionally' in this sense is not just about skill or competence or even conscientiousness, but something more specific. It is about playing the role that you signed up to when you joined the profession, and setting aside your own personal feelings and interests where they conflict with that role. We speak of soldiers being professional when they conscientiously perform a difficult role and do not run away, in spite of feelings of fear, horror and exhaustion. The need to be professional in this sense is very important in social work too, for social work often places us in positions that set off very powerful emotional responses: fear, rage, pity, disgust, shame, embarrassment. All these unpleasant feelings may make us inclined to behave in ways that will get us out of having to do things that we find difficult and distressing, even if they are necessary in the interests of carrying out our responsibilities to service users.

When we speak of professionalism in this kind of way, we are really speaking, not just about a person's outputs, but about a quality of the person themselves. In fact, one could say that we are speaking about a particular kind of *virtue* (to use the term that we introduced in Chapter 2), which is to do with 'the notion of the individual practitioner *committed to fulfilling their role*' (Banks and Gallagher, 2009: 147, our emphasis; see also Oakley and Cocking, 2001, on virtue ethics applied to professional roles).

Banks and Gallagher link professionalism in particular to the virtue of trustworthiness. Thus, referring back to the example in Exercise 6.1, you need to be able to *trust* your doctor not to gossip about things you have revealed in confidence; you need to be able to *trust* your doctor to carry out examinations of your body without this becoming sexual; and you need to *trust* that you will get the same standard of advice and treatment, regardless of the doctor's personal feelings about you as an individual. Professionalism also entails, among others, the virtues of courage and self-restraint, because it is easy in social work to slip into behaviour which is *unprofessional*, as Exercise 6.4 aims to illustrate.

EXERCISE 6.4

POSSIBLE PITFALLS

The following are examples of unprofessional behaviour which are quite easy to fall into. Which of these behaviours do you think you yourself are most likely to be prone to? Can you think of other kinds of unprofessional behaviour which you might be vulnerable to?

- Spending too much time on a particular case because you find the company of a particular service user rewarding.
- Failing to challenge a service user, or 'watering down' difficult messages, because you find the service user intimidating and wish to avoid making them angry.
- Failing to challenge a service user, or 'watering down' difficult messages, because you feel sorry for the service user and do not want to upset them.
- Telling service users about your own problems, perhaps out of a desire to demonstrate that you too are human.
- Colluding with service users against your own agency.
- Allowing your judgement to be swayed by service users or other professionals who you find powerful and intimidating.
- Promising more than you can really deliver out of a desire to prove your usefulness.
- Performing tasks for a service user that they could really do themselves, in order to win their gratitude.
- Acting in a punitive way towards service users whose behaviour you dislike.
- Acting in a punitive way towards service users who have been dismissive or critical of your work.
- Tolerating or condoning the unprofessional behaviour of others, in order to avoid making yourself unpopular.

Comments on Exercise 6.4

At one time or another, both of the authors of this book have probably erred in their own practice as social workers in quite a few of these ways, and we believe this would be true to a greater or lesser extent of most social workers.

One aspect of becoming a self-aware, reflective professional social worker, we would suggest, is being honest with yourself about your weak points. It is important to notice your own vulnerabilities and the situations in which they become apparent.

PROFESSIONAL ETHICS

We have seen that the word 'professional' includes a broad meaning of work competently and conscientiously done ('The builder did a very professional job on my extension'), and a more specific meaning of a role properly performed, regardless of the personal feelings of the individual involved. Both meanings imply work that adheres to certain standards, in the first case standards to do with competency, in the second case standards to do with integrity. If you look at the codes of practice of the various bodies that represent and/or regulate the various professions, you will see that they are concerned in various ways to maintain standards both of competence and integrity, and the same is true in the UK of codes of ethics that have been produced for social workers by the British Association of Social Workers (BASW, 2012), and the General Social Care Council (GSCC, 2010).

However, there are two aspects of social work practice which distinguish social work from most other professions. The first is that social workers by and large do not provide a universal service. Much of the population of the UK and other countries goes through life without ever making use of a social worker. Social work is a profession that specialises to a large extent in working with people who are in some way disadvantaged or excluded relative to society as a whole. It's appropriate, therefore, for reasons discussed in Chapter 4, that social work professional ethics should place a particular emphasis on social justice.

The second way in which social work differs from many other professions is that many of its service users are not service users by choice. The BASW code acknowledges this when it places a requirement on social workers to 'use the authority of their role in a responsible, accountable and respectful manner. They should exercise authority appropriately to safeguard people with whom they work and to ensure people have as much control over their lives as is consistent with the rights of others' (BASW, 2012: 13). As we will discuss in the next chapter, the ethical issues involved in the use of these kinds of powers are discussed less often than one might expect in the social work literature. All professions possess power by reason of their status and expertise, and professional ethics and codes exist in large part to try and prevent those powers from being abused, but social workers are in an exceptionally powerful position in relation to involuntary service users, who have no choice but to work with them.

ON THE RECEIVING END OF A CHILD PROTECTION INVESTIGATION

Suppose that you are a parent and that, for some reason, a neighbour reports you to social services and says (incorrectly) that you are mistreating your child. What would you, as the subject of the referral, expect to happen?

Comments on Exercise 6.5

We do not know what your expectations would be. For ourselves, we would like:

- to know that the referral had been made;
- to be consulted before any other agencies were approached;
- to know precisely how the matter had been left, including what records were being kept, and for how long, who had been informed about the referral and its outcome, and what had been said to them.

It is perhaps a little harder to decide how you would expect to be treated if you were behaving in a dangerous and irrational way.

BEING 'SECTIONED'

We hope that you never have the experience, but it is something that could happen to any of us. Suppose that you develop a psychotic illness or some other kind of delusional state which means that you become convinced that there is a world-wide conspiracy against you and your family. You believe that you can detect the people who are out to get you by 'listening to their thoughts' in the street. You decide that the best form of defence is attack and you inform your family that you intend to 'go after the enemy agents' and 'take them out by whatever means necessary'.

Neighbours contact the police and, as a result, community psychiatric services, including a social worker, become involved. This is in England, and part of the social worker's task is to decide whether you should be detained under the 1983 Mental Health Act.

How would you now wish to be treated if this eventuality should occur in the future?

Comments on Exercise 6.6

We suspect that you would want to be prevented from doing something that you might regret for the rest of your life. Probably you would agree that physical restraint might have to be used to achieve this. The traditional social work value of 'respect for persons' is not always synonymous with allowing people to make their own decisions. Sometimes it is right to protect people against their own impulses.

However, you would probably want the job to be done in a way that minimised the humiliation caused to you and ensured that, as far as you were able to understand, you were clear as to what was happening and what your rights were.

Probably you would also like to be sure that strong safeguards were built into the system used to detain you so as to prevent the misuse of this power. You would want to be sure, for example, that the power to detain you against your wishes only applied during times when you lacked the capacity to make your own rational choices. You would want to be sure that there were safeguards in place to ensure that those given power over you did not mistreat you.

REAL-WORLD CHALLENGES

In our comments on exercises such as 6.5 and 6.6 above, we try to draw out principles for practice. In real-life situations, though, it can be rather difficult to draw out and consistently apply such principles. For one thing, we are fallible human beings and there are all kinds of personal pressures that come to bear on us (in ways we explored in Exercise 6.4). For another thing, social workers operate in organisations that are also fallible and human, where there are always political pressures to act in ways that do not necessarily constitute best practice (as we discussed in the previous chapter). If your manager has a performance target to meet, for instance, she may be tempted to get you to do work that will help her to meet it, even if that work is not really the highest priority in terms of achieving the best outcomes for service users. (As Jane Green observes, 'the practices of performance management and managerial target-setting more often than not lead to perverse incentives which distort professional judgement' [2009: 116].)

As we will discuss in Chapter 10, every social worker, too, inevitably has to operate with finite resources and a finite number of hours in the week, which means being forced into making difficult choices and compromises that you might prefer not to have to make. For example, in our comments on Exercise 6.5 we said we'd wish to be informed about any referral made about us, but we suspect that many duty social workers dealing with situations like this will make checks with other agencies, and if satisfied that the referral has no factual basis, simply close the case, arguing that, if they took time to inform parents of the details of every such 'No Further Action' referral, they would have less time to perform other equally important tasks.

Quite apart from all these pressures and limitations, a major difficulty with drawing out universal principles of conduct is that each situation is unique, with every new situation potentially throwing up a new ethical dilemma, in which values or ethical principles are placed in conflict with one another in a new way. Ethical dilemmas of various kinds have been and will be discussed throughout this book. Here, for the present, are some examples of the kinds of ethical dilemmas that are commonly encountered in social work:

- self-determination *versus* welfare (this arises in situations such as that described in Exercise 6.6);
- valuing cultural diversity *versus* protecting individuals;
- the needs and wishes of a service user *versus* the needs and wishes of her carer;
- respecting confidentiality *versus* good inter-agency communication;
- self-determination *versus* the interests of the community;
- the needs of communities *versus* the needs of individuals.

EXERCISE 6.7

COMMON ETHICAL DILEMMAS

Looking at the six examples we have just given of types of ethical dilemmas that are commonly encountered in social work, try and think of examples of situations where these dilemmas might arise.

Comments on Exercise 6.7

The following are some suggestions, relating to various client groups. It should be possible to think of examples of dilemmas of these kinds arising in work with all client groups:

1 An adult man with a history of severe depressive illness insists, firmly and clearly, that he does not want treatment and does not want to enter a mental hospital. There is no reason to suppose he is a risk to others, but he has been getting increasingly depressed and has been increasingly expressing suicidal thoughts. He says people have a right to commit suicide if they wish. You are an Approved Social Worker trying to decide whether to apply for a section under the 1983 Mental Health Act.

2 A girl of Sudanese origin in the looked-after system (i.e. in public care) expresses a wish to visit relatives in the Sudan, who are able to pay for her airfare. As her social worker, you are aware that, in her community, genital excision of girls (illegal in this country) is regarded as normal and proper, and you suspect that the relatives intend to carry this out when she gets back there.

3 A physically frail elderly woman depends on her married daughter for all her personal care. She cannot safely get out of bed by herself, cannot manage stairs, cannot bathe and cannot get out of the house. She refuses to have any other help in the home and is adamant that she will never consider entering residential care. Asked what she would do if her daughter would not or could not help, she says she would have to manage somehow. Her daughter is exhausted and her own health is suffering as a result of juggling the demands of her mother with the rest of her life.

4 Following a child abuse tragedy, agencies in your area have been criticised for poor communication. To improve communication, a local school sets up a system of 'Early Warning' meetings, to which social services, the police and local doctors and health

visitors are invited, as well as social workers. At the meetings, the school produces a list of children who are causing them concern, and asks the other agencies to contribute what they know about these cases in order to build up a fuller picture and determine whether or not further action needs to be taken. You get to the meeting to find that a family you are working with is on the list. You know the parents have serious marital problems and that the father is receiving treatment for alcoholism, but what information should you share with this large group of professionals, some of whom have never met the family?

5   An eccentric elderly recluse lives in a house with no heating, running water or electricity, with a large number of cats. He draws water from a well he has dug in the garden, which is otherwise completely overgrown. He is very dirty and with long, filthy matted hair. He is verbally aggressive and will shout abuse and throw things at people passing in the street, but has never been known to actually harm anyone. Neighbours however say that 'something should be done about him' because he is frightening their children and posing a health risk.

6   You are a family social worker operating in an area of very high economic deprivation. A high percentage of families in the area are known to your agency because of concerns about child maltreatment, child behaviour and youth offending. Because of the community's experience of frequent intervention by social workers and frequent removals of children into public care, social workers are regarded with fear and suspicion in the area, as powerful agents of an oppressive state. How do you follow up (as you must) on new referrals about child maltreatment, without further contributing to this feeling of oppression and thus to the general demoralisation and low self-esteem which is probably a factor in the high incidence of family problems?

Every profession is faced with ethical dilemmas. Ethical dilemmas in medicine, in particular, are frequently in the news. In some ways, though, social work is unique because it is in a paradoxical position. More than any other profession, it traditionally identifies itself with those who are oppressed or marginalised by society, yet it is created, sustained, directed and funded by that same society, and largely by the state. Likewise, while the profession is encouraged to work in partnership with service users (e.g. Department of Health, 2000: 12), a large part of its brief – particularly in work with mentally ill people and children and families – is to impose and police certain socially agreed norms, if necessary resorting to the law to compel compliance (as we will discuss further in the next chapter).

LIMITATIONS OF CASES AND CODES

Sarah Banks has rightly expressed concerns about the overuse of 'ethical dilemmas' and case studies as a means of teaching professional ethics. As she points out, 'the focus in professional ethics textbooks on difficult cases makes it seem as if "ethical issues" only arise when a problematic or difficult case arises' (2009: 57; see also Banks and Williams, 2005). She has similar doubts about focusing too much on written codes of ethics, which can result in 'an image of "ethics" as being about conformity to rules and standards' (2009: 56). What she is resisting, it seems to us, is a view of 'professional ethics' as being quasi-legal: a matter of rules and their application in practice.

It is important to have rules as a benchmark against which misconduct can be measured, but we hope that this chapter has demonstrated that professional conduct is about a great deal more than simply adherence to rules, or the ability to 'solve' ethical dilemmas as if they were mathematical problems. One of the characteristics that mark out 'professionals' is that they are not simply functionaries, who can do their job adequately simply by following routinised procedures laid down by others. The status of 'professional' comes with roles that involve making difficult judgements for which you are responsible yourself, and for which you can be held to account. It also comes with power and authority, and this can only be exercised in an ethical way by someone who is 'in submission … to a set of values that he [or she] chooses to uphold' (Davies, 2009: 324), even in situations where to do so is painful. The important point that Hazel Davies is making here is that ethical practice resides, above all, in a personal commitment, not just in knowing a list of rules. In other words, she is referring to a kind of virtue. As Chris Clark observes, 'professionals have undertaken a special obligation to learn, practice and live the virtues that animate professionalism in their own specialized sphere' (2007: 73–4).

CHAPTER SUMMARY

This chapter begins the second part of the book in which we look at issues that arise in practice. In it we have discussed why ordinary ethical standards are not necessarily sufficient in a work context because of the particular relationship that exists between professional and service user. We have explored the nature of 'professionalism', including the idea of professionalism as a kind of virtue. We have looked at professional ethics in general, and the particular issues that arise for social work. We have discussed the challenges that are thrown up in the real world to any attempt to set out general principles for practice. Finally, we have discussed the limitations of using case exercises and ethical codes as a framework for learning about ethical practice. Important as codes of conduct may be as a benchmark, professionalism is, in the end, a quality that an individual professional possesses, rather than a set of rules.

 FURTHER READING

We would recommend the following books to those interested in thinking further about the nature of professionalism:

Banks, S. and Gallagher, A. (2009) *Ethics in Professional Life*. Basingstoke: Palgrave.
Oakley, J. and Cocking, D. (2001) *Virtue Ethics and Professional Roles*. Cambridge: Cambridge University Press.

7

POWER AND CONTROL

- Social work power
- Facing our power
- Care and control
- Abuse and misuse of power
- Recognising powerlessness

In the previous two chapters, we have on a number of occasions referred to the power which social workers have in relation to their service users. This chapter will discuss the ethical issues arising from the use of power, and, in particular, from the use of the kinds of coercive powers (that is: powers to control, if necessary by force) which are distinctive to social work.

SOCIAL WORK POWER

All professionals, to varying degrees, have power resulting from their social status, their real or perceived expertise, and their position as gatekeepers to services and resources. In terms of status and perceived expertise, social workers tend to have rather less power than, say, doctors or lawyers, and can sometimes feel rather powerless in relation to these other professions. However, many social workers also exercise a different kind of power, one that derives from the legislative frameworks within which they work. Social workers in the children and families field, for instance, may, if they think it necessary to protect a child from harm, go to court to request a care order or an emergency protection order, which will allow them to remove a child from a family. Since these social workers can enlist the support of the police if necessary, such orders mean that families can be physically compelled to hand over their children. Social workers in Youth Offending Teams also exercise power on behalf of the courts: young people may be required to meet them regularly for supervision, for instance, or face a return to court and a possible custodial sentence. Another group of social workers who may use coercive legal powers in England and Wales are those acting as Approved Mental Health Professionals under the 2007 Mental Health Act, who may, under some circumstances, decide that people should be detained in hospital against their wishes. Again, this may be enforced, if necessary, with the support of the police. These kinds of coercive legal power, over and above the kinds of power that social workers share with other professionals, are a striking and distinctive characteristic of social work as a professional activity.

What is not always sufficiently recognised is that the power derived from legislation extends far beyond the situations in which legal powers are actually formally invoked. As Michael Sheppard points out, the supportive, collaborative side of social work does not exist 'in some vacuum, insulated from the more authority-based coercive powers' (2006: 106). Referring in particular to child and family work, he goes on to say:

> Even where social workers are carrying out their tasks to support the family, with every intention of maintaining the child with their family, their authority role remains. The potential for ... coercive action can hang like a sword of Damocles over the conduct of their practice ... There is clear evidence that parents are well aware of the ... coercive powers of social workers, and that this has a major impact on the way that many of them behave ... Indeed there is evidence that some mothers find it difficult to recognise that social workers are carrying out supportive functions ... because they are so overwhelmed by the more coercive powers which are held by social workers, should things not go right ... The emotional stakes are so high and the potential powers so great that they practically define the nature of social work intervention. (Sheppard, 2006: 106. The evidence referred to is from Sheppard with Kelly, 2001, and Thoburn, 1995)

Sheppard makes a distinction between 'overt coercion', which occurs when social workers use legal powers to exercise control over events, and 'latent coercion', which is the power (described above in Sheppard's words) that social workers have as the result of public knowledge of the existence of those legal powers. Most families, for instance, will allow a child protection social worker, without any kind of court order, to enter their houses and check their children's bedrooms or kitchen cupboards, even though the social worker cannot legally insist on doing so. Paul Spicker makes the same point by using an analogy:

> Normally, within the context of preventative work with families, the social worker acts by persuasion, negotiation and nominal agreement; but parents who are under supervision know that if they do not co-operate with the social worker, the social worker may be able to initiate procedures which will lead to control. It is absurd to pretend that the parents have much choice. They have nothing more than the freedom of the sheep to run from the sheepdog. As long as the sheep continues to run in the right direction, the dog does nothing, but simply runs alongside. If the sheep looks like running off the line, the dog runs a little closer. If the sheep veers off in the wrong direction, the dog runs faster and barks. Are we really going to pretend that the sheep is self-determining? (Spicker, 1990: 225)

Latent as well as overt coercion is not confined to child and family social work. 'All mental health professionals, including social workers,' write Jim Campbell and Gavin Davidson, 'routinely use coercion with clients' (2009: 251), and they go on to discuss a whole spectrum of ways in which coercive power is exercised:

> These ... include a range of informal approaches from persuasion, through leverage (often described in terms of the withholding of services in response to non-compliance or offering rewards for compliance), to the use of direct demands or threats, as well as formal frameworks for coercion such as Guardianship, CTOs [Compulsory Treatment Orders] and compulsory admissions to psychiatric hospitals. (2009: 252)

A combination of overt and latent coercion (or 'formal' and 'informal' coercion as Campbell and Davidson call them) means that in some sectors of social work, including the sector that in the UK employs the most social workers (child and family work), *most* service users are not really voluntary clients, but work with social workers because they feel they have no choice.

The existence of these powers to coerce has huge implications for the nature of the relationship between social workers and their clients. And like all power, social work power has the potential to be abused or misused.

FACING OUR POWER

In the spirit of the 'duty of realism' discussed in Chapter 5, it seems to us that our first step, when thinking about the use of these powers, must be to try and be honest with ourselves about their extent. Some social workers can be rather squeamish about the power they wield, and reluctant to discuss it with service users. Others become too fond of power, and even boastful about it, worryingly desensitised to its effect on themselves and others. Child and family social workers participating in a focus group in which Chris Beckett was involved,

> ... talked in a shocked and disapproving way of a social worker in another team who said to a client with a snap of the fingers: 'I can take your baby away just like that.' The anecdote showed an extreme expression of social workers' power, and they wanted to distance themselves from it. (Taylor et al., 2008: 26)

Such a crass and bullying expression of power is indeed shocking and ugly, and shows a really worrying lack of self-awareness. However, the opposite approach of pretending to service users that you are on an equal power footing with them is also unacceptable because it is dishonest. If we are not clear with service users, albeit in much more respectful terms than those just cited, about the powers that we may in some circumstances call upon, then we are deceiving them about the nature of the working relationship. If we ourselves refuse to think about the power we have and its implications, then we are deceiving ourselves.

Kerstin Svensson suggests that social workers tend either to 'ignore' their controlling role, or to 'separate' from it (by describing it as belonging to the organisation in which they work, or to the courts, rather than themselves), or to 'rewrite' it in more benign terms. She argues that if we do not keep asking questions about what social workers actually *do*, as opposed to questions about how we prefer to describe ourselves, 'there is a risk that social work will contain much more control than we are aware of' (Svensson, 2009: 246). And if we cease to even be *aware* of the power we have, we will not be in a good position to determine whether or not we are using it appropriately. It is worth remembering that the misuse of power is often more visible to those on the receiving end, than it is to those exercising it, for, by and large, the powerless try and keep on the right side of those who have power over them, and tend not to complain.

CARE AND CONTROL

Many texts speak of social work's dual roles of 'care', on the one hand, and 'control' on the other, as if they were different, even opposite things. Pamela Trevithick, for instance, refers to 'conflicting responsibilities' (2000: 140), but the exercise of coercive power is not necessarily an uncaring act. In social work, as in life generally, care and control are not necessarily in conflict. We would not, for instance, consider a parent to be very caring if they did not exercise control over their toddler's behaviour next to a busy road.

In situations where people are unable to take full responsibility for their own safety because of lack of understanding (as is the case with small children and roads), a professional duty of care must extend to exercising some control over them. Residential social workers regularly exercise this kind of caring control in respect of children or vulnerable adults in their care. Similarly, in situations where people are at risk due to their own lack of power, professionals with a duty of care may need to exercise control over *others* in order to protect them. If you think about the situation of a child who is being sexually abused by a parent, or a frail and confused old person who is being bullied or robbed by a carer, you will see that, in both cases, human beings are suffering because of their own almost total powerlessness relative to those who are supposed to be looking after them. Social work power, used appropriately, simply redresses the balance. There are situations, too, where control of service users is exercised in order to protect the public. This is one of the aims of the youth justice system, and is one of the reasons for detaining people compulsorily under mental health legislation.

So 'control', when used appropriately, is not the opposite of care, but on the contrary is an expression of care. We should not fall into the trap of thinking that the use of statutory powers is necessarily 'oppressive' or that working in other ways is necessarily anti-oppressive. It would not have been an oppressive act, for instance, if the child protection agencies had intervened to remove 'Baby Peter'

Connelly from his mother's care before he died in such horrific circumstances in 2007 (BBC News, 2011a).

Nevertheless, a number of dangers exist for social workers operating in contexts where the use of coercive powers is part of their brief:

- *Desensitisation.* Frequent use of statutory powers may easily desensitise us to the seriousness of them. We may end up forgetting what a traumatic event it can be to be detained in a hospital against your wishes, or to be taken into care. There is also quite a strong human tendency to distance oneself from those with whom one is in conflict. When we exercise power over others against their wishes, this can coarsen our relationship with them, and lead us to become dismissive, disrespectful or even contemptuous.
- *Meeting our own needs.* The exercise of power can even become a pleasure, a way of bolstering our own sense of importance, and this may lead us to exercise power in situations where it is not necessary, or to flaunt power, like the social worker cited earlier, who snapped her fingers and said 'I can take your baby away just like that,' or even to frankly abuse it. Power can be seductive and even addictive. It can also be used unnecessarily to allay our own insecurities and fears of losing control, or even to 'punish' a service user we have experienced as difficult and challenging.
- *Power as a 'quick fix'.* The fact that we can resort to these powers may tempt us to do so, even in situations which could in fact be much better resolved, given time and patience, by negotiation, trust building and mutual agreement.
- *Cumulative negative effects of power.* The more that statutory powers are used, the greater the potential for social workers to become objects of fear in the communities where they work, thus eroding the trust that is required if they are to be able to work in supportive and non-threatening ways.
- *Discrimination.* We may be inappropriately influenced – in one way or another – in our decisions about the use of statutory powers by factors such as the ethnicity of the service user. Neil Thompson notes the 'over-representation of black people in "control" situations and under-representation in "care" situations' (2006: 79). On the other hand, the Climbié report (Laming, 2003) discussed the possibility that the professional *failure* to intervene may have been partly the result of fears of seeming racist, given that Victoria and her aunt were of African (Ivorian) origin. (In this case, the inquiry ultimately concluded that this was *not* a factor.)
- *Reluctance to exercise power appropriately.* Although there are many reasons why power might be unnecessarily used, there is also an opposite danger that we may fail to use statutory powers in situations where a vulnerable person is in need of protection, perhaps because we are afraid of, or sorry for, the one who the vulnerable person needs protecting against. A need to be liked, a need not to be seen as the 'bad guy', may contribute to this, as can a general lack of confidence that makes us uncomfortable about assuming authority. To fail to exercise coercive powers when it is appropriate to do so, is, in its own way, as unethical as it is to use them unnecessarily. Think of a policeman who failed to intervene to prevent an assault, or a schoolteacher who tolerated bullying in the classroom.

The following exercise invites you to consider the ways in which you yourself might run into difficulties of these kinds:

YOU AND POWER

Imagine yourself in a social work job which includes, as a substantial component, the use of coercive powers (child protection, mental health, youth justice). We have suggested above a number of ways in which bad practice can occur in that context. Given that we all stray into bad practice, in which of the ways listed above are you most likely to err?

In order to answer this question, you may need to consider how you operate in other areas of life – and the feedback you get from other people.

For instance:

- Do people ever accuse you of being a 'control freak'? Are you ever impatient with others who take longer than you do to make decisions? Or are you the sort of person who prefers to let others take the lead?
- Are you aware of being someone who tries very hard to be liked?
- Do you enjoy the business of thrashing things out with people you have had differences with, or do you find this rather difficult and anxiety-provoking?
- Do you tend to avoid confrontation, or do you relish a fight?
- Are you easily intimidated by angry or hostile people?

Comments on Exercise 7.1

Looking back over our own practice as social workers, we can think of instances where we erred both in the direction of failing to step in when it would have been better to do so, and in the opposite direction of seeking too quickly to take control and impose a solution. Either way, our own anxieties about losing control, on the one hand, and about getting into conflicts, on the other, will have played a part in our thinking.

ABUSE AND MISUSE OF POWER

Dictionary definitions indicate that the words 'misuse' and 'abuse' have overlapping meanings: both refer to the improper use of a thing. For us, 'misuse of power' implies power used inappropriately but not necessarily with malign intent, while 'abuse of power' refers to the deliberate use of power by someone in a powerful position for his or her benefit or gratification. However, the words are often used interchangeably, and indeed 'misuse' and 'abuse', even defined in our terms, are not completely separate things, but part of a continuum. At one end of the spectrum is a social worker habitually turning up late to appointments with a service user who is not powerful enough to make a fuss about the inconvenience caused. (Smith [2008: 3] devotes a whole section of his book on power in social work to 'the power to be late'. If you think lateness has nothing to do with power, ask yourself if you would be more or less likely to be ten minutes late for an appointment with a consultant paediatrician than you would for an appointment with a service user.) At the other end of the spectrum is a social worker who physically or sexually assaults vulnerable service users for his or her own gratification, knowing they will be too scared to complain.

The following list of ways in which power can be inappropriately used is based on Wilding (1982), though we have adapted it for our own purposes:

- *Excessive claims to expertise.* Professionals sometimes overstate their expertise. An example would be if you were to assert that, 'in your professional opinion' something was undoubtedly true, when in fact you did not have the evidence to make such a dogmatic assertion. There have been cases of miscarriages of justice arising from other professionals making excessive claims of expertise in the courtroom (for example, the case of Sally Clark, convicted of murdering her baby son on medical evidence that is now thought to be unreliable [BBC News, 2007]). The misuse of power here consists of a professional getting his or her own view to prevail over the views of others on grounds which are in fact spurious. As Donald Schön noted:

  > Whenever a professional claims to 'know' in the sense of the technical expert, he imposes his categories, theories, and techniques on the situation before him. He ignores, explains away, or controls those features of the situation, including the human beings within it, which do not fit his knowledge-in-practice. (Schön, 1991: 345)

- *Exaggerated claims of influence.* It can also be tempting to exaggerate your influence. For example, social workers sometimes promise that they can provide a certain service when in fact the decision is ultimately not theirs to make. They may also mistakenly give reassurances which they are not really in a position to give.
- *Failure of responsibility.* This occurs where professionals have not properly carried out the duties entrusted to them. If, for instance, a social worker were to fail to carry out checks on a case as required under child protection procedures then this would be failure of responsibility and could of course result in a child being avoidably harmed. (Sometimes it is impossible, for resource reasons, for a social worker to carry out all the duties that she has been given. In these circumstances, the social worker's duty is surely to make it clear to her employers that this is the case. It would be failure of responsibility not to draw attention to the problem.)
- *Abuse of position.* This arises where professionals use the power accruing to their professional status for purposes other than the best interests of service users. A fairly extreme example would be that of a social worker who used the feeling of intimacy generated by one-to-one sessions to seduce a vulnerable client. There are many other more subtle ways of abusing power which most of us have probably at some time been guilty of.
- *Disabling 'help'.* This is 'help' that has the effect of undermining the confidence of service users in their own capabilities and occurs when social workers do things for service users

which they could actually do for themselves. What is particularly insidious about this sort of abuse of power is that the social worker and the service user may both see it as helpful (for instance, a service user may be grateful to a social worker who sorts things out for her, but may in the long run lose out if this means that she never learns to sort things out for herself).

- *Undermining personal responsibility.* This is really a specific kind of disabling 'help', which occurs when professionals undermine their client's sense of responsibility for their own actions. Exercise 8.4, in the next chapter, will give an example of this. (The exercise can be found on page 112.)
- *Neglecting rights.* Again, this may happen in situations where professionals sincerely believe that they are acting in the interests of service users. For instance, a service user's right to confidentiality, or right to be consulted, or even a service user's right to make mistakes may be bypassed by professionals who believe that they are doing so for the good of the service user.

The following exercise asks you to consider how social workers might misuse their power in each of these seven ways:

EXERCISE 7.2

THE MISUSE OF POWER

Try and come up with one example, for each of the above categories, in which social workers might misuse their power. Try not to think of extreme examples, but of examples which might be encountered on an everyday basis. In particular, we suggest that you try and think of examples that you could just about imagine being guilty of yourself.

Also ask yourself the following: in which circumstances is misuse of power of this kind most likely?

The seven headings are:

- Excessive claims to expertise
- Exaggerated claims of influence
- Failure of responsibility
- Abuse of position
- Disabling 'help'
- Undermining personal responsibility
- Neglecting rights

Comments on Exercise 7.2

The point we wish to make here is that misuse of power is not necessarily some monstrous thing that other, very wicked, people do, but something that any social worker is capable of unless he or she is vigilant. This is why it is worth thinking about which kinds of misuse of power you yourself are most vulnerable to – and in what circumstances.

You may agree that the following circumstances make misuses of power more likely to occur:

- We may be tempted to make excessive claims to expertise at times when our own expertise feels under threat or when we are carried away by our subjective feelings. (For instance, if you have a strong hunch that a child has been sexually abused, you may be tempted to say 'In my professional opinion there is no room for doubt that this child has been abused', even if in fact you do not have incontrovertible evidence and could be wrong.)
- We may make exaggerated claims to influence when we are anxious to placate a service user who is angry or distressed, or when we ourselves are secretly doubtful as to whether we have anything useful to offer.
- Failure of responsibility can result either from complacency or from being preoccupied with other things. It can result too from shortage of time or lack of support, though the responsibility of the social worker then becomes one of drawing attention to the problem and being honest about what can and cannot realistically be done.
- Social workers have abused their position in some appalling ways, as we can see from cases where workers in residential children's homes have physically and sexually abused children. But that is at the extreme end of the spectrum. There are many ways of abusing your position which it is quite easy to fall into, such as using your professional status to impose your view of things over the view of a service user. For example, if you were defending yourself against a complaint by a service user, you might use your status and your communication skills to win the argument. We suspect these sorts of petty abuse of power are more common than social workers might like to admit, and arise particularly in situations where we feel insecure and vulnerable.
- We may be tempted to provide disabling 'help' sometimes because it seems quicker and easier. We may also be tempted to do it when we want to bask in the gratitude of the service user.
- Undermining personal responsibility is something that a social worker is very unlikely to set out deliberately to do, but can quite easily do inadvertently. It may result from a desire to be liked and to avoid confrontation. It is often easier to be 'understanding' than to be 'challenging', though good social work requires both.
- Neglecting rights may occur in a variety of circumstances. Sometimes the effort of consulting a service user (particularly if the service user is difficult to deal with in some way) may seem too much trouble. It may be tempting simply to bypass the service user. Sometimes we may persuade ourselves that the 'end justifies the means' in a given situation. Social workers often rationalise being dishonest with service users (which really means neglecting their right to accurate information) on the grounds that being completely honest would 'harm the working relationship'. This is often more about the social worker wishing to avoid discomfort, however, than about the service user's needs.

We argued in Chapter 4 that the policies which social workers are required to implement are seldom developed with the sole purpose of improving the lives of service
users: there are almost always other agendas involved. Likewise, professional bodies, whose ostensible aim is to maintain professional standards and provide the best
possible service, have their own agendas in that they tend to seek to enhance the
power, status and working conditions of their members. In our commentary on
Exercise 7.2, we have tried to show that these multiple agendas are at play even at
the individual level. Each of us as an individual human being, while trying to act
'professionally', also has his or her own personal agenda which will influence our
actions and may, if we are not careful, lead us to misuse power. Honesty and self-
awareness are therefore vital. It would be naive and dangerous to assume that our
own actions are necessarily beyond reproach, simply because of the job we do. Yet
some professionals do behave as if this really were the case. Writing from the perspective of the parents' group, PAIN, Sue Amphlett observes:

> During their training, childcare and protection workers are taught the child is their cli-
> ent and their only concern must be to act in the best interests of the child. Consequently
> the mantra for many of them is, 'We are working in the best interests of your child.' As a
> consequence many of them truly believe that they cannot be the cause of any harm to a
> child. (Amphlett, 2000: 175)

We have our own hidden agendas, sometimes hidden even from ourselves. Simply
saying – or believing – that we only act in the best interests of service users does not
necessarily mean that this is really the case.

RECOGNISING POWERLESSNESS

In the board game Monopoly, players attempt to acquire property in order to accumulate rent from other players. It is, in a way, a simple representation of a capitalist
society such as the UK. But, in one respect, Monopoly is very much fairer than real
life: in the game, all the players start off with an equal sum of money. Few people
would bother to compete in a game of Monopoly in which another player was
allowed to start out with ten times more money, for the outcome would be almost
a foregone conclusion. That player would, in effect, have all the power. In real life,
though, some start out with money, education, social connections, ability and personal confidence while others start out with none of these things – and yet no one
really has the option of refusing to take part in the game.

In another respect, Monopoly is rather tougher than the real world. In the game,
the losers end up with nothing at all. In the real world, there is a safety net, albeit
a very imperfect one, in the form of a benefits system, social housing, free schools
and hospitals, and a variety of other public services, one of which is of course
social work.

But what function does social work play in the real-life game of Monopoly?
Looking at it optimistically, social work helps those who are losing out, equipping

them to rejoin the game with a better chance of holding their own. But there is a more pessimistic way of looking at it. Perhaps social work is not *really* there for those who are losing out. Perhaps (as we have discussed previously in this book) what social work really does is to serve the interests of those who are *winning* the game by making it look as if those who are losing are doing so because of their own individual failings, and not because of the unfairness of the game itself?

Social workers regularly encounter people whose problems are, in large measure, the result of circumstances that they feel unable to change: in other words, people who experience themselves as having very little power. When thinking about the use and misuse of power by social workers, we need to bear in mind that those on the receiving end of misuses of power are typically people who are exceptionally power*less*.

JULIE'S HOME-ALONE CHILDREN

EXERCISE 7.3

Julie is a lone carer of three small children aged 9, 5 and 2. She has a lot to cope with. She has big financial worries and has several thousand pounds of rent arrears which were run up by her ex-partner, Hugh, who had an expensive drug habit. It was not unusual for Hugh to spend most of the family's weekly income on his habit.

Julie also has debts to pay off to fuel companies and several hundred pounds owing which she borrowed to pay for the children's Christmas presents.

Julie lives in fear of violence from Hugh, who resents the fact that she ended the relationship and comes to the house on a regular basis to make threats, ask for money or demand to be allowed to return. He often beat her when he was living in the house, and getting him to leave was very difficult and took a great deal of courage. He still lives locally and boasts that he has friends in the neighbourhood who watch over Julie's every move. Julie herself has few contacts in the area. She grew up in care and has no contact with her own family.

Julie badly wants to move with the children to a new area, but there is no question of a housing transfer until she has managed to clear the rent arrears.

However, she is offered the opportunity of a cash-in-hand job, working nights, within 15 minutes of her house. It would allow her to make some surplus money to pay off debts, and work towards a housing move and the new start which she believes is in her interests and those of the children. She has no one to leave the children with, but she teaches the older child how to contact her by phone, and takes the risk of going out at night to work, leaving the children alone in bed.

Unfortunately for her, this is reported to Hugh by one of his friends and Hugh reports her to the authorities. When Julie admits to regularly leaving the children alone at night, there is a full child protection investigation, involving social services and the police, on grounds of neglect.

What are your thoughts on Julie's behaviour (assuming that all the above information is accurate and can be corroborated)? What should be the professional response?

Comments on Exercise 7.3

Obviously, it is dangerous to leave such small children on their own, and the child protection agencies cannot just ignore this behaviour.

However, Julie's behaviour was not motivated by malice or lack of care for the children. It was a desperate attempt to remedy a dire situation which was largely not of her own making. A woman with more money, or one who did not have the misfortune to have taken up with a partner who turned out to be violent and to have a drug habit, would never have needed to contemplate taking such a step, and therefore would never have had her competence to parent called into question.

A professional response which did no more than castigate Julie's behaviour would, it seems to us, be oppressive and a misuse of power. An appropriate response would have to acknowledge the difficulties that Julie was facing (how well would the rest of us do, if placed in her shoes?) and try in some way to support her in resolving her debt, her constant fear of violence and her conviction that a move to another area would give her and the children a new start.

In order to act or to change, people need to feel that they have some power. If the effect of exercising social work power is to increase people's feeling of powerlessness, then we cannot expect the intervention to help them to change. It would be like telling someone to win more often at Monopoly, while simultaneously reducing the amount of money they had to play with. Somehow social workers need to use their own power in a way that does not disempower their clients, but if possible empowers them. It is a difficult task.

CHAPTER SUMMARY

In this chapter, we have looked at the powers that social workers have, and particularly those based on legal coercion. We have noted that social workers are sometimes rather reluctant to admit to the scale of these powers, but suggested that it was important to be honest, both with service users and ourselves, about their extent. We went on to discuss the 'care and control' aspects of social work, arguing that these are not necessarily opposites as some suggest, and that control is in some cases necessary if we are to care for and protect vulnerable people. We considered different attitudes to exercising control and the effect of power on those who exercise it. We then discussed the abuse and misuse of power. Finally, we drew attention to the fact that social work powers are typically exercised in respect of people who are among the most powerless in society, and pointed out that people need to feel they have some power in order to be able to act and change.

FURTHER READING

We included in this chapter a lengthy passage from the following book, which is not all about power, but includes an interesting chapter on 'Authority and choice':

Sheppard, M. (2006) *Social Work and Social Exclusion: The Idea of Practice*. Aldershot: Ashgate.

The following book provides more information about power and social work than we have been able to offer here, including much more on the nature of power itself:

Smith, R. (2008) *Social Work and Power*. Basingstoke: Palgrave.

Several articles cited in this chapter appeared in a special issue of the journal *Ethics and Social Welfare*, into which both authors of this book had some editorial input:

'The Ethics of Control' (2009 Special Issue), *Ethics and Social Welfare*, 3(3).

8

SELF-DETERMINATION AND PRIVACY

- What does self-determination really mean?
- Positive and negative freedom
- The pressure to control
- A sense of responsibility
- Consumer choice and service-user power
- Individual or group
- Privacy and confidentiality versus information sharing

In this chapter, we will look at the social work profession's traditional commitment to the principle of self-determination, which Lynne Healy defines as 'respecting and facilitating the ability of the client to make his or her own life choices and decisions' (2007: 18). The principle of service user self-determination was one of Biestek's seven casework principles (1963), modified versions of which, as Sarah Banks notes (2006), were widely adopted by writers on social work ethics in the 1960s and 1970s, and continue to be influential. The idea of respecting the self-determination of service users remains very much a feature, not only of social work discourse but also of government, with its recurring emphasis on 'choice and independence' (Carr, 2007). The contrast will be obvious, however, between this chapter and the previous one, in which we looked at the overt and latent coercion exercised by social workers to compel people to do things.

A similar tension exists between the emphasis on inter-agency information sharing that is such a hallmark of modern social work practice and the principle of respecting privacy and confidentiality. We will come back to this later in the chapter.

WHAT DOES SELF-DETERMINATION REALLY MEAN?

The Code of Ethics of the British Association of Social Workers defines its first 'basic value' – 'Human dignity and worth' – as follows:

> Social workers should respect, promote and support people's dignity and right to make their own choices and decisions, irrespective of their values and life choices, *provided this does not threaten the rights, safety and legitimate interests of others.* (BASW, 2012: 8, our emphasis)

In a similar vein, the National Association of Social Workers in the USA states the following, under the heading of 'Dignity and Worth of the Person':

> Social workers treat each person in a caring and respectful fashion, mindful of individual differences and cultural and ethnic diversity. Social workers promote clients' *socially responsible* self-determination. (NASW, 2008, our emphasis)

One thing you may notice about both of these statements is the way that self-determination is hedged with caveats: self-determination should be respected, but only as long as it doesn't harm others, and is socially responsible. In a sense this is obvious, and applies not only to social work service users, but to us all. Our own rights and freedoms have to take into account the freedoms and rights of others, and none of us would expect to be allowed to do whatever we like, regardless of the consequences to other people. But since, as we've seen in the previous chapter, risks to themselves and others are the rationale for a whole range of restrictions imposed on social work service users, we might well ask what the principle of self-determination really means in the social work context, if it can so easily be over-ruled. As Sarah Banks observes:

> self-determination can mean all things to all people, from maintaining that each individual should be completely free to do whatever they want (a version of negative freedom …), to justifying fairly large-scale interventions from the state to enable individuals to become more self-determining or self-realising (a version of positive freedom …). (Banks, 2006: 33–4)

'Self-determination', it seems, is in danger of being yet another of those comforting buzzwords we discussed in Chapter 5, which we all agree to be a 'good thing' without really examining what we mean by them, and without really noticing that different people may in fact use the words in different, contradictory or even opposite ways.

POSITIVE AND NEGATIVE FREEDOM

The distinction that Sarah Banks made in the quotation above between 'negative' and 'positive' freedom (Berlin, 1997 [1958]) is a very fundamental one which it is important to get hold of.

Negative freedom refers simply to the absence of constraints: it means not being stopped from doing whatever it is you want to do. Positive freedom is about promoting the ability to determine one's own life. You can see how different the two ideas are, if you consider the parenting of small children. Most parents would wish to teach their children to make their own decisions and take charge of their own lives (positive freedom), but few parents would think that the best way to achieve this would be to allow their children to do whatever they wanted, watch TV whenever they felt like it, eat whatever took their fancy, and skip school whenever they chose (negative freedom). In other words, most parents would agree that to achieve positive freedom for children, you need to set some limits to their negative freedom. If you don't restrict a small child's negative freedom next to a busy road, for instance, they could have a fatal accident and end up with no freedom at all. If you allow a child to eat whatever and whenever he likes, he may become obese, which will close down all kinds of options that he might otherwise have had. If you allow a child to use addictive drugs, she may end up being a slave to a habit that will dominate her life, and restrict her ability to do anything else at all.

Adopting a 'positive freedom' angle on self-determination, Michael Sheppard (2006) goes as far as to argue that there need be no contradiction at all between social work's exercise of coercive power, and its commitment to self-determination: if we restrict people's choices now in order to enable them to make better choices for themselves in the future, we are actually *supporting* self-determination.

However, this assumes that we social workers are impartial and omniscient arbiters, who will always know the right thing to do and always do it, rather than being the flawed human beings that we actually are, ourselves subject to pressure, constraint and self-deception. Most people would agree that a society needs to defend negative freedoms (for example, the right to free speech, which allows its citizens to say even foolish and unpleasant things) in order to protect us from those in authority who might otherwise seek to control us in the name of some greater good. Go too far down the road of restricting negative freedom in the name of promoting positive freedom, and we could end up in the world of George Orwell's *Nineteen Eighty-Four* (2004 [1949]), where one of the great slogans of the totalitarian state of Oceania was 'FREEDOM IS SLAVERY'.

Indeed, is it not the case that we need some negative freedom, if we are to develop positive freedom at all? Can we really learn how to direct our own lives, if we are always protected against our own mistakes? As David Soyer observed in a paper entitled 'The Right to Fail', making mistakes 'is how all people grow, how they gain a more mature view of themselves and the world. They succeed and fail and through success and failure they learn' (1963: 77).

THE PRESSURE TO CONTROL

CONCERNS ABOUT MRS MOORE'S SAFETY

You are a social worker working in adult social care. Your client is Mrs Moore. She is 91 and lives by herself in a narrow terraced house with a steep staircase. She is physically very frail, and is subject to blackouts, which have resulted in her having a number of nasty falls requiring hospitalisation. Support at home is being provided by your agency, but does not provide the round-the-clock care that would be needed to eliminate this risk. Her GP and her daughter (a woman with young children who lives 40 miles away and visits twice a week) have both expressed the view that Mrs Moore is no longer safe at home and should be moved to residential care for her own good. In fact, her GP states that it is not just possible, but actually likely, that if she remains at home she will have a fatal fall. Both the doctor and the daughter are aware that Mrs Moore herself is reluctant to move, but they maintain that she is rather confused, and needs, in her own best interests, to be persuaded to go.

Mrs Moore is a little forgetful and vague, but is not suffering from dementia, and when asked about whether she thinks she ought to go into a home, her view is as follows:

> 'I know that I could have another fall, and I know it could kill me, but when you get to my age, you don't worry so much about how long you're going to live. I'd rather risk a nasty fall, if it means dying in my own home, than move into one of those homes, which I know I'd hate.'

When you relay this back to the daughter, she says firstly that her mother is mistaken:

> 'She's never liked change, but once she's moved she'll be fine.'

She then adds that other people's needs should be taken into account:

> 'In a way I think my mother's being selfish, and not thinking about me. I worry all the time about her having a fall. How would it reflect on me, if I let my own mother live on her own in a terraced house, and she had a fall and died? And for that matter, how would it reflect on social care?'

The GP, who is a rather aggressive and domineering man, is quite blunt. In a letter addressed to you, he states:

> 'In my professional opinion, Mrs Moore will die an unpleasant death if you don't act. I suggest that you and your agency think very carefully about whether you wish to ignore this opinion, and take sole responsibility yourselves for the inevitable outcome when it occurs.'

What should you do?

Comments on Exercise 8.1

One response to this might be to argue that any such outcome would not be your responsibility, or your agency's, for in fact you have not refused to provide residential care. On the contrary, you have offered it, and it has been declined by the service user herself, who is an adult capable of making her own choices. (After all, social workers are not expected to intervene when younger adults decide to engage in activities that place them at risk of fatal injury.)

On the other hand, you may feel that her daughter is right. Perhaps, if Mrs Moore were to try it, she'd find she liked residential care better than she expected. You might even have some sympathy with the view that Mrs Moore is being a little selfish. It isn't only her who is being affected by her choice to stay at home.

It is possible that, even if, deep down, you think that Mrs Moore should be allowed to remain at home if that's what she wants, you might still be vulnerable to the feeling that you will be blamed if Mrs Moore were to have an accident in her own home, and may therefore still be inclined to persuade yourself that she should move. Perhaps in such circumstances, you might tell yourself that you were actually supporting Mrs Moore's self-determination, in that you would be making it possible for her to live a fuller life, with more social contact and more opportunities, than she has when confined to her home?

Social workers are often under pressure, from neighbours, from family members, from other professionals, from their own agencies – and even from their own fears and doubts – to overrule service users' wishes, using either latent or overt powers, and even in situations when the social workers themselves have doubts about whether such a step is justified (see, for instance, Malcolm Kinney, 2009, on the pressures on a social worker to 'section' someone under the 1983 Mental Health Act). There is therefore an ever-present danger that the perceptions, wishes and rights of service users will end up being set aside for the wrong reasons. The idea of positive freedom can unfortunately rather easily be invoked as a justification in such circumstances. We might, for instance, justify cajoling Mrs Moore (in the exercise above) to go into residential care against her wishes, by persuading ourselves that in the long run she would be happier there, feel safer and feel more confident about making choices, even if our real motive for doing it was to stop us having to deal with the pressure from relatives and neighbours, and to reduce our own anxieties.

In other situations, though, we may be reluctant to intervene when in fact we should, and we may use the idea of negative freedom as a rationalisation for inaction, even when, in fact, it is not the real basis for our reluctance to take a firm line.

WORKING WITH THE JENNINGS FAMILY

You are working with the Jennings family, which consists of Mr and Mrs Jennings and their children, Tom (5) and Lisa (4). Compared with many of the families you work with, Mr and Mrs Jennings are very welcoming. They say you are the best social worker they have ever had, always have the kettle on ready when you visit and always (ever since you mentioned they were your favourite) have a packet of chocolate Hobnobs ready.

However, their care of their children is poor. The children are often dirty and smelly. There are persistent reports that the children are allowed to play in the street unsupervised, in spite of fairly heavy traffic, that they are often inadequately dressed in cold weather, and that Mr and Mrs Jennings sometimes leave them on their own in the house. At other times, they leave them in the care of a large number of different babysitters, some of them young teenagers who ought to be in school.

You are under pressure from neighbours and other professionals to 'do something' about this poor, and potentially dangerous, parenting, and to consider calling a child protection conference on grounds of neglect. It is pointed out to you that you have been visiting the Jennings for some time and, although Mr and Mrs Jennings maintain that you have been a great help to them, they never actually change. But you are very reluctant to do something that will distress Mr and Mrs Jennings too much, and spoil the pleasant relationship you now have with them.

What rationalisation might you find yourself using to justify inaction?

Comments on Exercise 8.2

Of course, you may feel that you would not be so weak as to try and rationalise inaction if action was necessary, in which case good for you, but we wonder whether you might be tempted to at least delay a decision by (for instance) persuading yourself that Mr and Mrs Jennings were doing what was right by their own standards, and telling yourself that it was not your place to impose conventional middle-class standards on them. 'They aren't deliberately harming their children,' you might decide, 'and it's not up to the nanny state to tell them precisely how they should care for them.' If so, you'd be evoking the Jennings' right to negative freedom as a justification for not placing more pressure on them to change.

What we have tried to show is that self-determination can be a rather slippery concept, which we can use to rationalise both intervention and non-intervention. Because self-determination can be taken to mean *either* supporting positive freedom *or* supporting negative freedom, we can often rather too easily claim to be acting in its name *whatever* course of action we take.

And yet we do *need* both ideas – positive *and* negative freedom – even though they are in tension with one another. As a general rule, positive freedom is particularly important in situations where people do not have the full capacity to make informed choices, such as is the case with young children: we can probably all agree that children need to be supported in learning how to make decisions and take responsibility for themselves. On the other hand, in cases where people do have that capacity, then negative freedom becomes more important. When people are capable of making choices, and understanding the consequences of those choices, then what justification can there be for making choices for them, unless, of course, their choices are harmful to others?

But capacity itself is a difficult concept, debatable in every given instance, and there are many grey areas. René Bergeron, for instance, argues that even an adult with full mental capacity is not always truly in a position to make real choices about her own life, particularly when 'depressed, or sick, or abused' (2008: 88). Writing about elderly people, she observes that 'months or years of abuse, or neglect, or being financially exploited' may 'leave a victim feeling that his or her situation was not solvable, even by a trained professional … [and] depression may make the simplest change seem insurmountable' (2008: 88–9). She cites the example of a woman ('Dolly'), who had been subjected to emotional and sexual abuse over a long period by her husband. Two years after a professional intervention which had eventually removed her from the abusive situation, Bergeron asked Dolly if it had been right to put her safety above her right to self-determination:

> [Dolly's] response was quite direct and clear. 'How dare you professionals speak of self-determination when I was obviously suffering?' She explained that she was incapable of telling anyone about the abuse as it was happening because of her feelings of shame and that the abuse was her fault for marrying him. She also stated she could not effectively evaluate choices offered because she did not feel she deserved anything more than what she was getting from her husband. She said her isolation greatly impacted her perspective and that what she needed was immediate distancing from her situation, at least initially, before she could effectively make her own decisions. (2008: 89)

This was an adult with no obvious impairment to her mental capacity, and yet Bergeron makes a persuasive case that this was a situation where going *against* the client's wishes was actually the best way to support genuine self-determination, for it was only when she was out of the abusive situation that she felt able to make any decisions at all.

A SENSE OF RESPONSIBILITY

It is commonly said that with freedom comes responsibility. Adults make decisions for small children when they are not old enough to make decisions for themselves, and this is reflected in the fact that small children (under the age of 10 in England and Wales, though this varies from country to country) cannot be convicted of a criminal offence. As we grow older, we are given more freedom to choose, but we are expected to take more responsibility. In fact it is difficult to see how a society could function in which people were granted freedom to act, but were not held responsible for the consequences of those actions. And perhaps, when we speak about promoting self-determination in the 'positive freedom' sense, what we are talking about is encouraging the development of an ability to *take responsibility*. Encouraging people to take responsibility can sometimes result in our deciding to act in ways that, in the short term, might seem counter to our service users' own best interests.

LIAM'S UNPAID RENT

Liam, aged 17, moved into a supported housing project for young people run by a housing association, having had some difficulties at home, and a brief spell in residential care. He got a job in a fast-food restaurant, but started getting into trouble with the manager for turning up late. Staff at the project offered to try and help him sort things out with the manager, but he declined the help, and lost the job. He obtained a Job Seeker's Allowance to live off, but in order to pay his rent, he now needed to apply for housing benefit. He didn't take the necessary paperwork to support his application, and was told to come back with it. He failed to do so, and therefore could not pay his rent.

Staff at the project, and his social worker too, repeatedly reminded him about this, warning him that if he got too far in arrears with his rent, he'd be evicted from the project. Liam still didn't go back with the paperwork, even after a review meeting attended by his parents, his Connexions worker and his social worker, where he was again reminded of the importance of getting his benefits sorted out, and the risk of eventual eviction, and even though everyone present offered to help him sort it out if he was finding it difficult. The housing association initiated its eviction procedures, which involved him being sent a series of warning letters. Eventually, he received 28 days notice to quit.

At this point, Liam appealed against the decision. He said he didn't want to leave, and that he needed more time. An appeal hearing was arranged. He was advised by his social worker to get on with sorting out his benefits so that he would be able to demonstrate at the hearing that he'd done something, but at the hearing he had still got no further with his benefits claim. What ought to happen now?

Comments on Exercise 8.3

You may well feel you'd like more information before forming an opinion on this. (Is Liam very depressed? Is he illiterate? Does he have a learning disability?) However, what we think the exercise demonstrates is that the principle of self-determination involves rather more than simply giving people whatever they want.

(Cont'd)

> At the present moment, what Liam wants is for the threat of eviction to be lifted. That, at present, would be his choice. But in fact, over a period of some time, he has himself been making a series of choices not to do anything to prevent the need for eviction (alternatives have repeatedly been offered to him). So perhaps the most useful lesson he could learn from this is that, in adult life, choices really do have consequences. In this case, it might actually be in Liam's interests, and not just the interests of the housing association, for the eviction to go ahead.

Of course, in many cases, it is rather obvious that service users' actions are in part a consequence of their circumstances, how they have been treated, and what they have been given the opportunity to learn, and this does make it difficult to know how to get the balance right between insisting that people take responsibility for their own choices, and giving due acknowledgement to the constraints and pressures they were under when they made bad decisions in the past.

EXERCISE 8.4

REASONS FOR BEN'S OFFENDING

You work in a Youth Offending Team and have been writing a court report on a young man called Ben, who is accused of a series of offences of theft. If Ben is found guilty, your report will be used by the judge when deciding what sentence to pass. You are aware that this young man has had a very unhappy childhood. From an early age, it seems, he has been abused, rejected and ignored. Throughout his life, Ben's parents have always had other priorities than Ben himself. It seems to you that he has every reason to feel angry with the world.

Ben asks to see the report you have written about him. When he sees it, his first comment is this:

> 'So you're saying I couldn't help myself, right? You're saying it's not my fault that I steal stuff. It's because of my mum and dad.'

How do you respond to this?

Comments on Exercise 8.4

Social workers tend to look for explanations for things and – rightly – try to avoid making moral judgements about those they work with. Explanations are useful in a situation like this. Clearly, it would be simplistic and unjust simply to characterise Ben's problems as being no one's fault but his own.

But Ben's question highlights a difficulty. In offering explanations for things, we are in danger of undermining people's sense of being in charge of their own lives. Although Ben might be glad to be offered someone else to blame for his problems, in the long run it is not going to be terribly helpful to him to see all the fault as lying with other people.

So some care is needed when considering how to answer Ben's question. Perhaps something along these lines:

'No. You could help yourself. You could have decided not to steal. I'm just pointing out to the judge that you may need a bit of help to see that.'

CONSUMER CHOICE AND SERVICE-USER POWER

We have referred earlier to the emphasis on *choice* in contemporary political discourse. Indeed, one might argue that, as well as negative and positive freedom, there is now a third conception of self-determination, which we might term 'consumer freedom'. If negative freedom is about not restricting people's choices, and positive freedom is about acting to enhance people's ability to *make* choices – the difference between the two is well illustrated by the example from Bergeron (2008) above – then we might characterise 'consumer freedom' as being about making the maximum number of options available for service users to choose between. We live in an age in which, for some time, all the major political parties in the UK, the USA and many other Western countries have accepted, almost as a given, the notion that the marketplace should, as far as possible, be the means through which people obtain for themselves the goods and services they want or need. This approach has its drawbacks, as Peter Scourfield observes:

A danger of using independence and choice as central organizing principles is to forget how and why the public sector emerged in the first place – to ensure that those who are necessarily dependent are treated with respect and dignity, to ensure a collectivized approach to risk, and to ensure that secure and reliable forms of support outside of the market or the family are available. (2007: 108)

He goes on to caution that a social care system in which service users choose, recruit and manage their own services, could end up with a situation where 'the quality of service someone receives is less to do with what needs they have and more to do with their entrepreneurial competence' (2007: 119–20). Ian Ferguson suggests that:

the combination of poverty, multiple discrimination, a lack of resources in every sense and (frequently) physical or mental impairment means that the typical user of social work services will often not match Ulrich Beck's description of the 'choosing, deciding, shaping human being who aspires to be the author of their life' and who, he tells us, 'is the central character of our time'. (2007: 396, referring to Beck, 1999: 9)

In Britain, at the time of writing, this kind of 'consumer freedom', in which the service user is encouraged to choose, purchase and manage his or her own services, is an integral part of the policy agenda that goes under the name of 'personalisation' (another term, incidentally, which, as Ferguson [2007] warns, is in danger of becoming one of those 'all things to all men' buzzwords). In fact, personalisation's enthusiasts see the concept as extending well beyond the provision of direct payments. Charles Leadbetter, for instance, suggests that it includes the possibility of involving service users in a much more fundamental way, not simply as consumers, but as 'co-designers and co-producers of a service' who 'actively participate in its design and provision ... because they want to find solutions that do not leave them dependent upon the state' (2004: 24). Beyond that, he suggests (in an idea that has echoes of 'The Big Society' espoused by the British Prime Minister, David Cameron), lies the possibility of 'the public good emerging from within society', with professionals helping 'to create platforms and environments, peer-to peer support networks, which allow people to devise these solutions collaboratively' for themselves (Leadbetter, 2004: 24).

You may notice that Leadbetter's idea of personalisation actually includes two quite distinct and separate elements which he has merged together as if they were one and the same: first, the idea of service users having a choice about their own services, and second, the idea of 'solutions that do not leave them dependent on the state'. The progressive, humane agenda that is suggested by the first idea (for who could be against the idea of service users having a say about their own services?) serves as a kind of window-dressing for the second idea, which is the traditionally right-wing preoccupation with rolling back the state (an idea associated, for instance, with the ultra-conservative Tea Party in the USA, whose supporters equate state welfare provision with tyranny [see, for instance, Frank, 2012]). All of us in the UK are service users of the state-funded NHS, and British readers might like to ask themselves if they feel 'dependent' on the NHS, whether abolishing the NHS would enhance their self-determination, or whether, on the contrary, access to publicly funded health care is itself an important kind of freedom.

Once again, we see that self-determination and choice are very complicated and even slippery ideas, which can be called upon to justify all sorts of different courses of action, at the policy level as well as at the level of case-by-case decision making.

INDIVIDUAL OR GROUP

This chapter would be incomplete if we did not acknowledge that the particular conception of self-determination and individual freedom that now exists in the industrialised countries of North America, Western Europe and Australasia is culturally specific. It is possible to debate how much freedom there really is in these countries, and how evenly freedom is distributed among their citizens, but it is surely true to say that in all of them the *idea* of freedom, or liberty, is accorded very high esteem. Remember that 'Life, liberty and the pursuit of happiness' are the inalienable rights of man as defined in the American Declaration of Independence, that the motto of the French Republic is 'Liberty, Equality, Fraternity', and that Britain, in the famous patriotic song, is the 'Land of hope and glory, mother of the free'.

As we have seen, in political discourse in contemporary Britain, 'choice', another word closely related to freedom or self-determination, is assumed to be self-evidently desirable. Whether people necessarily want more and more choice in these areas is a question that is seldom even raised.

But this isn't how things have always been seen and it isn't how they are seen in every culture today. The liberal values that place such importance on individual freedom, are values that have risen in capitalist society, a form of society which by its nature creates economic inequality. Bill Jordan (1991) has even suggested that social work's liberal values – such as the idea of individual self-determination – may actually be at odds with its social justice values, such as the commitment to 'duty to challenge social conditions that contribute to social exclusion, stigmatisation or subjugation, and work towards an inclusive society' (BASW, 2012: 9).

Different cultures do not always place the same value on the autonomy of the individual as it is given in the West, and may draw the line in different places between the rights of the individual and the rights of the community or group. Writing about the applicability of the idea of self-determination to Africa, and specifically to Zambia, Geoffrey Silavwe comments: 'When "man" or "woman" is defined only as a member of a group then "self" is defined as within the group as well. In such a situation ... the closest one could get to the practice of self-determination is group self-determination' (Silavwe, 1995: 72).

We need to be aware therefore that the exceptionally high value given to individual self-determination in the West is not necessarily given to it by people with roots in other parts of the globe where, for instance, community solidarity or family cohesion may be seen as more important, and 'group well-being' may be valued 'above individual desires or self-gain' (Bergeron, 2008: 86). We would not wish to overstate this. Even in countries like Britain or the USA, as we have seen, the right to self-determination is not absolute and can be 'trumped' by many other considerations, including the needs of the wider community. So, differences between cultures are differences of degree. Nevertheless, serious misunderstandings can result from assuming that people of every culture view these matters in the same way. René Bergeron, for instance, suggests that elder abuse may go undetected, if workers take Western cultural assumptions about individual autonomy, and apply them to people from other cultural backgrounds:

> If the elder's cultural background has been authority driven by family or the community, self-determination will not be feasible from an individual perspective. These victims may need strong guidance throughout the decisional process. (2008: 94)

PRIVACY AND CONFIDENTIALITY VERSUS INFORMATION SHARING

The tension between, on the one hand, respecting privacy and confidentiality and, on the other, inter-agency information sharing, is an important instance of the wider tension between respecting individual self-determination, and imposing solutions in the best interests of individuals and society. In fact, privacy is a negative freedom, the freedom to decide who knows your business and who doesn't.

Recent events in the UK have highlighted the issue of privacy. Most people were shocked to learn, in 2011, that tabloid newspapers were routinely 'hacking' into private phones (see, for instance, Chandrasekhar et al., 2011), feeling that people's purely private lives should be protected against such intrusion. And yet, in many areas of social work, you will find highly sensitive pieces of personal information about service users – their relationships, their sex lives, their mental health, their consumption of alcohol and drugs, their feelings about their children or their parents – being recorded on files to which many people have access, and passed between one agency and another, there to be re-recorded in more files, and perhaps passed on again.

There are good reasons for this, of course. Information sharing between agencies is not the same thing as press intrusion into private lives, for the rationale behind it is to ensure that risks don't go unnoticed. In the child protection field in particular, inquiry after inquiry has identified poor information sharing as a problem. But surprisingly little attention is given to the downside of this: it represents an infringement of what most people would regard as their privacy, and of the kind of confidentiality that most of us expect from professionals. (Consider, for instance, what you would expect from a counsellor or therapist in terms of confidentiality.) It is also likely to erode trust, to the point that people are less willing to confide in professionals in the first place. Imagine you are a parent and you are suffering from depression. Would you be more or less likely to seek the help and advice of your GP, if you thought the GP would inform children's social care, than you would if you thought the GP would not do so?

Worried about the possible loss of trust, some professionals, including social workers, simply do not tell their service users that what they say may be passed on to others. An Australian social worker, interviewed by Helen McLaren, justified this failure to forewarn clients by saying: 'If someone felt that we might breach confidence and it got out that the service was not completely confidential no one would come to see us' (2007: 30). This seems a pretty dubious strategy, first because it is dishonest, and second because in the long run it is almost certain to be counterproductive. The client will find out in due course that the social worker has passed things on, and this will result in greater distrust than would have occurred if the social worker had spelled out to her in the first place the ground rules of their working relationship, and the circumstances under which information given in confidence would need to be passed on. (And of course, it will also 'get out' that social workers are tricksy people, who pass on information which you thought you'd told them in confidence: service users do talk to one another.)

Other social workers admitted to McLaren that they didn't forewarn service users because it made *them* feel uncomfortable. 'They would just look at me and think I am some hard-nosed social worker that is not really there for them', observed one (2007: 31), calling to mind the observations made by Kerstin Svensson (2009), quoted in the previous chapter, about the way that social workers tend to deceive themselves about the extent of their 'controlling' role, and distance themselves from their responsibilities as employees of social work organisations, in order to protect their sense of themselves as 'good'.

JANE, WHO WANTS TO CONFIDE IN YOU

You are visiting a lone mother, Jane, who is having difficulty coping with her 5-year-old son Jack, and has herself asked for help. Jane is very isolated and is desperate to talk to someone she feels she can trust. 'You've got a kind face,' she says, 'thank God for that. I feel I can talk to you.' This was not a child protection referral, but you know that, in the event that the mother discloses to you anything that suggested to you that the boy is at risk in her care, you will have to pass this on to others. What should you tell the mother at the outset about the confidentiality you can offer?

Comments on Exercise 8.5

This is exactly the kind of situation in which you might be tempted not to tell Jane about your duty to report child protection concerns. You (like some of the social workers interviewed by Helen McLaren) might feel that such a warning would sound a jarring note at the beginning of an interview in which you want to come over as supportive and helpful. You might also wonder whether, by telling her this, you would inhibit her from telling you anything at all.

But consider what would happen if you said nothing to discourage Jane from thinking that she could talk to you in complete confidence, and later on she said something which made you feel you had to initiate child protection procedures. Her sense of betrayal will be much greater than it would have been if you had been frank with her in the first place about the fact that you couldn't offer her unconditional confidentiality. If you had been clear with her, you would be able to refer back to your earlier conversation and remind her that you had not misled or deceived her.

What you will need to do is develop a way of being honest with people about ground rules in a way that does not come over as too alienating or bureaucratic, but at the same time does not 'beat about the bush', or distort or minimise the true situation. In our experience, service users greatly appreciate honesty, even if they don't like what you say. If you think about it, we suspect that you will agree that this would be what you would want also, were you to become a social work service user yourself.

Our suggestion here is that clarity about the limits to confidentiality is essential from the outset in meetings with service users. We cannot in the long run expect to win people's trust by deceiving them. But there is a broader debate too, which cannot be addressed case by case, but to which social workers can contribute as citizens, about the balance between privacy and state surveillance. It is part of the wider issue of the balance between, on the one hand, the right to self-determination in the 'negative freedom' sense, and the need for public agencies to intervene in private lives in order to protect the vulnerable. As is often the case with ethical questions, there is no final right answer to this because there is more than one principle involved. (As Isaiah Berlin put it, 'human goals are many, not all of them commensurable, and in perpetual rivalry with one another' [1997 [1958]: 241].)

In an article written shortly before her current fame as the architect of reforms to the British child protection system, Eileen Munro criticised the (then) government's enthusiasm for increasingly high levels of information sharing between agencies. Although she is writing specifically about confidentiality, the following extract serves quite well as a more general warning that we should be careful about using positive freedom as a pretext for eroding negative freedom too far:

> 'Power corrupts' is a well-known truism but there is no acknowledgement of the possible danger of increasing state power over families. There is no recognition of the fact that liberal societies have placed a high value on privacy and confidentiality precisely because they present an obstacle to the state. While the state sees this in a negative light, the individual values it as a protection of their freedom. (Munro, 2007: 54)

CHAPTER SUMMARY

Self-determination has long been regarded as a key social work principle, but at the beginning of this chapter we asked what it really meant, when social workers are so often involved in overruling the choices of service users. We went on to discuss the key distinction between negative freedom (the absence of restrictions or controls) and positive freedom (a capacity to direct one's own life).

We discussed the frequent pressures on social workers to impose control on others, and discussed how social workers might concede to such pressures, and rationalise this by appealing to the idea of 'positive freedom'.

We then looked at the need to encourage a sense of responsibility, and discussed the implications of this when working with people who had made bad choices for understandable reasons. And we considered the current interest in consumer choice as a model for social care and public services generally, as well as the notion of services run by or designed by service users themselves.

We noted the different emphases made by different cultures regarding the balance of individual freedom and the needs of the community or group, and noted that errors of judgement might be made by social workers who were not sensitive to these cultural differences.

Finally, we discussed the tension between privacy and confidentiality, on the one hand, and information sharing between professionals and agencies, on the other.

 FURTHER READING

Although it is now more than half a century old, and the language somewhat dated, Isaiah Berlin's 'Two Concepts of Liberty' is still very helpful for those wishing to disentangle the different and even contradictory ideas that are entwined within the notion of self-determination, freedom or liberty. It can be found in the following book:

Berlin, I. (1997[1958]) *The Proper Study of Mankind.* London: Chatto and Windus.

9

RESPECT VERSUS OPPRESSION

- What is oppression?
- Levels of oppression
- Not simply victims
- The internalisation of oppression
- Oppression, objectification and 'respect for persons'
- Oppression and discrimination
- 'Minimal intervention'

The terms 'anti-oppressive' and 'anti-oppressive practice' (the latter often abbreviated as 'AOP') have been used so frequently – even *obsessively* – in social work education, that they are in danger of losing their meaning entirely and becoming more of those virtuous-sounding words that we use without really thinking what they mean, simply because we think it is what is expected of us. As Wilson and Beresford observe, 'AOP has become one of social work's sacred cows' (2000: 554).

Since social workers undoubtedly deal with people who experience oppression, and since social work is certainly itself capable of being very oppressive in its own right, oppression is very definitely something that social workers need to take seriously if they are to claim to practise in an ethical way. The first step towards doing so, though, is perhaps not so much to do with learning about 'anti-oppressive' theory, as it is about trying to get some insight into the experience of oppression itself. Some readers of this book will not find this hard: they will have plenty of experience of oppression at first hand to draw upon.

For others, though, such insight will require more imagination. If so, it is an effort that needs to be made. A social worker who has unthinkingly taken on board the lazy negative stereotypes of (for example) travellers, welfare claimants or asylum seekers, and never tried to look at the world from the position of the people who carry these labels, is, to put it politely, not well placed to work in a positive way with people from those groups. In fact, to be a social worker without some grasp of the nature and effects of oppression would, in our opinion, be a bit like being a doctor without a grasp of the nature and effects of bacteria. 'Oppression' and 'anti-oppressive practice' may have become irritating social work clichés, but oppression itself is certainly real enough.

'Respect', we suggest, is the other side of the coin. Properly applied, it seems to us, the principle of 'respect for persons' amounts to roughly the same thing as 'anti-oppressive practice'. Oppression involves denying a person respect, and as such, is at the heart of most kinds of unethical practice.

However, there is a *structural* element to oppression which has to be included in our understanding, if respect is not to be a hollow pretence. Arguing for an 'anti-oppressive ethics', Derek Clifford and Beverley Burke explain that:

> The point of adding the descriptive term 'anti-oppressive' to qualify 'ethics' is to empha-sise individual behaviour as inseparable from the unequal political and social contexts in which it occurs ... Although we accept that ethics is peculiarly related to individual personal responsibilities, for behaviour ..., situations involving social difference and inequality between people are the areas where issues of personal ethics become critical. (Clifford and Burke, 2009: 16–17)

WHAT IS OPPRESSION?

Oppression

Oppression: 'prolonged cruel or unjust treatment or exercise of authority ... [or] mental pressure or distress ...'.

Oppressive: 'inflicting harsh and authoritarian treatment: [as in] an oppressive dictatorship [or] weighing heavily on the mind or spirits ...'. (*Oxford Dictionary of English*, 2009)

The word 'oppression' means different things to different people. To some, perhaps, it conjures up images of slavery or apartheid or medieval despotism, and it may seem to be stretching things to equate the term with the circumstances of most users of social work services, who may be struggling with difficulties of one kind or another, but are not subjected to the slave driver's whip, or imprisoned for failing to carry a pass, or burnt at the stake for subscribing to the wrong religion. Many service users themselves might object to the word 'oppressed' being applied to them, even if they do feel weighed down upon. There is no reason why we should try (for instance) to describe an elderly couple as oppressed just because they are finding life hard and feel the need to ask a social services department to make an assessment of their social care needs.

Nevertheless, in any social work office, you will see people who are very obviously poor and downtrodden. A large proportion of service users – especially in some client groups – are living in inferior housing, on low incomes, with little or no work opportunities, in an environment where crime is a risk many times higher than the national average. Many too belong to groups which are stigmatised and discriminated against. So the word 'oppressed' does seem to us to be a fair and accurate word to use for a good many social work service users, though some might prefer to say 'hard put upon', 'disadvantaged', 'deprived' or 'socially excluded'. There are of course more derogatory words than these and we regret to say that if you look in social work files you may come across some of them – 'inadequate', for instance, is one particularly unpleasant word that was once quite commonly used in files to describe people – a reminder that social work, for all its 'anti-oppressive' rhetoric, is quite capable of being oppressive in its own right.

Not all social work service users are economically deprived, of course. Some are even wealthy. But all service users belong to groups which are, at least to some extent, in a marginalised position in society: disabled people, people with mental health problems, people with drug and alcohol problems, elderly people, children and parents who are struggling with family life. The problems experienced by all these people are not simply of their own making, but are linked to the attitudes and responses of society at large. The following exercise illustrates what we mean by this:

IS DANNY 'OPPRESSED'?

When he started secondary school, Danny could still barely read and write. (Neither of Danny's parents could read or write either, so they weren't in a position to help him.) The school was in an area where there were serious problems with recruiting teachers and a chronic shortage of staff, so that a lot of the teaching was done by a constantly changing stream of supply teachers, who tended to be preoccupied with managing difficult behaviour in the classroom, of which there was a lot, rather than teaching. There were a lot of people with problems in the area and it was a neighbourhood with high levels of unemployment and poverty.

In this context, Danny's literacy problems were not really picked up on, nor was the fact that he never completed homework. He had almost no contact with teachers, just sat at the back of the class waiting for it to finish. Classes were incredibly tedious. The day passed unbearably slowly as he waited for each hour of incomprehensible talk to go by. Classes were also humiliating. They made him feel stupid, which is what some of the other children called him. Danny had always been a bit clumsy and awkward with other children; not a complete loner, but always on the edge of things.

After about a year, he was surprised and flattered to find that a certain group of boys were prepared to take him on as a member of their group. These boys missed a lot of school which at first Danny found shocking, but when they asked him what he got out of school, he had

(Cont'd)

EXERCISE 9.1

to admit it was absolutely nothing, so he started missing school too. Notes went home to his parents, but nothing else happened.

Danny and his new friends started to miss more and more school and to get involved in increasingly reckless adventures. Pretty soon, Danny was involved in vandalism, shoplifting and taking and driving motor vehicles. He started getting caught. He became known to the police. The Youth Offending Team became involved.

Would you describe Danny as oppressed? If so, why?

Comments on Exercise 9.1

We think 'oppressed' is a reasonable word.

He has now acquired the label of a young offender, a criminal, and yet there is no reason to believe that this was some sort of in-built part of his nature.

The educational system failed him. This is not necessarily the fault of individual teachers, but a problem caused by the fact that the school was not adequately resourced to cope in the environment in which it was located. Teachers did not have time to notice Danny as an individual or to pick up on his problems, and as a result school became a tedious, humiliating, pointless ordeal.

In this context, it is not surprising that he was attracted to truancy and then to crime. It was a chance to be someone, to feel that he was actually doing something daring and exciting, and not just sitting around feeling like a fool.

The inadequacies of the education system cannot be blamed for 'making him a criminal' – he has to take some responsibility for his choices – but it can certainly be blamed for making this choice attractive and for not offering any alternatives that would feel meaningful.

LEVELS OF OPPRESSION

In the above exercise, we talked about Danny as an individual, but the oppression experienced by Danny – if you prefer, you could call it 'deprivation' or 'disadvantage' – is likely, to a greater or lesser degree, to be experienced by the entire community in which he lives. There are limited opportunities (high unemployment, high poverty) and the local secondary school, for whatever reason, is clearly not meeting the educational needs of all its pupils. It is quite likely that there will be similar problems with other local services, and that many other people in the community will also be oppressed (or deprived, or disadvantaged, if you prefer those words) in one way or another. 'Individuals have commonalities as well as differences,' as Clifford and

Burke put it (2009: 20). People's life chances are affected by their context, and that context, for some, includes 'lack of employment … institutional discrimination … unequal distribution of wealth and income … stereotyping in the media, and many other factors' (2009: 20).

Oppression, in other words, isn't just something that happens to certain individuals. It happens to *groups*. Allowing areas of 'deprivation' to develop and failing to provide adequate resources to allow those areas to recover – or their inhabitants to move on – is a way in which society at large oppresses certain sections of the population. In this case, the section of the population involved is the inhabitants of a particular neighbourhood, as well as the social class to which they belong. But groups defined in other ways – by gender, for example, or by ethnicity or age – also experience oppression of one kind or another.

OPPRESSIVE BEHAVIOUR BY SOCIAL WORK AGENCIES

EXERCISE 9.2

Can you think of ways in which a social work agency's behaviour might constitute oppression in relation to:

(a) people from poor working-class backgrounds;
(b) women;
(c) black people?

Comments on Exercise 9.2

You will have thought of other examples, but here are three that occurred to us:

- Our impression is that social work and other agencies share with one another confidential information about poor working-class people in a way that would not be tolerated if it was the norm in a prosperous middle-class community.
- Society expects women to be carers, but does not place the same expectations on men. Informal women carers of elderly or disabled people – daughters, wives, daughter-in-laws – may be placed under pressure to cope with extremely demanding and completely unpaid work in order to save service departments from having to pay for care.
- An example of the way agencies can be oppressive to black people is provided by Neil Thompson (2006) who comments that black and ethnic minority people are more likely to be subjected to legal coercion than white people, as demonstrated by disproportionate numbers of black people who are compulsorily detained under mental health legislation, or receive custodial offences, or are in care (he cites Ahmad, 1990, and Barn, 1993, among others). Eileen Munro notes that professionals may be more inclined to initiate a child protection response to families identified as black, than they would to families in identical circumstances who are not so identified (2008: 79, citing Birchall and Hallett, 1995).

In many cases, the oppression of groups is structural, which is to say that it is built into the way society itself operates. Keating (1997) offers a multidimensional model, on similar lines to Thompson's 'PCS' model (2006) which we discussed in Chapter 3, to clarify the different levels at which oppression occurs. The dimensions, or levels, he proposed are the 'socio-political', the 'socio-cultural' and the 'psychological'. The 'socio-political' level is the level at which 'oppression is legitimated and institution-alised' and the level at which power is used to 'dominate and assign differential status to groups' (Keating, 1997: 36). The 'socio-cultural' level is the level at which oppression is transmitted and propagated in society. At this level, oppression is mediated through language and the way we 'construct meaning' (1997). Keating points in particular to the way in which we define difference, which is one of the cornerstones upon which oppression is built. (Consider the ideas and assumptions that have been built up around the term 'asylum seeker' in modern British society and you begin to see how this works.) The 'psychological' level refers to the ways in which an individual is affected by oppression and to the ways in which those experiences impact on that individual's life.

If we see oppression only at the psychological level, without recognising all its socio-cultural and socio-political underpinnings, we may end up laying responsibility for the psychological effects of oppression upon the affected individual themselves, rather than seeing those effects, at least to some degree, as a response to external circumstances, as was surely the case with Danny in Exercise 9.1.

NOT SIMPLY VICTIMS

One danger in recognising that certain groups are oppressed, though, is that we can end up thinking of whole categories of people – even sentimentalising them – in the passive role of 'victims' in need of rescue or enlightenment by social workers. Anne Wilson and Peter Beresford, for instance, cite with approval Sibeon's (1991) critique of Dominelli and McLeod's book, *Feminist Social Work*:

> [Dominelli and McLeod, 1989] refer to the 'misery' of women, their 'plight', their 'servi-tude' and their mistaken sense of 'contentment'. Women who experience contentment are wrong to do so: they do not perceive they have 'real' or 'objective' interests *qua* their status as women. (Sibeon, 1991: 19–20, as cited by Wilson and Beresford, 2000: 561)

Sibeon's objection here is to a way of talking about women that makes them sound like passive victims who do not even understand their own situation. 'On this account,' Wilson and Beresford observe, taking up Sibeon's point, 'there would appear to be little room for service users' own knowledges' (2000: 561) and the 'power to define and construct service users remains with the social work practitioners and academics – however "radical" they may be' (2000: 561). This, they point out, is not so very different from older approaches that preceded 'anti-oppressive practice'. Wilson and Beresford's position is that it is ultimately the oppressed themselves who know best what oppression is actually like.

It is also important to remember that an oppressed person does not cease to be a moral agent, capable of doing good and bad things, and that people who are oppressed *may themselves act oppressively*. Oppression isn't something that is only practised by the overtly powerful, or by those who hold positions of authority. We all have the potential to be both oppressor and oppressed. As Franz Fanon asserts, 'at one time we may be oppressed, whereas at another, we may be the oppressor' (Fanon, 1967, cited in Keating, 1997: 10).

Among the most clearly oppressed in society are children living in grossly neglectful or abusive situations. To be in a situation where you are abused but have no means of escaping from that situation because of the huge power differences between you and your abuser, is surely a 'textbook case' of oppression in terms of the two definitions we gave earlier. The difficulty that social workers often face is that abusive or neglectful parents are often themselves from oppressed groups (though, of course, by no means always: there are abusive and neglectful upper-class parents too). When this is the case, the social worker has to be careful not to let her concern to avoid acting oppressively towards the parents distract her from the harm that may be done to the child in the parents' care. It is equally important that she does not allow her concern to protect the child to provide a pretext for acting oppressively towards the family as a whole, or ignoring the structural oppression which the family as a whole may be up against. Not only would this be unjust to the parents, but ultimately it would be unhelpful to the child.

THE INTERNALISATION OF OPPRESSION

One of the crueller aspects of the psychology of oppression is the way that the oppressed tend to 'internalise' their own oppression. In fact, this internalisation is an important part of the way that an oppressor maintains domination and control. An example is the way in which an abused child who is constantly told she is worthless and deserving only of abuse may herself come to believe this: worthlessness and being deserving of abuse become part of her self-image. This also occurs with many women who are subjected to abuse by their partners (Harne and Radford, 2008), and the same sort of process occurs with whole groups. Subjected repeatedly both to oppression itself and to the belief system of the oppressor, people can come to believe their own oppression is actually justified. In his autobiography, the former South African president, Nelson Mandela, gives an example of this when he describes his momentary feeling of panic when, on boarding an aeroplane, he noticed that the pilot, like himself, was black:

> We put down briefly in Khartoum where we changed to an Ethiopian Airways flight to Addis. Here I experienced a rather strange sensation. As I was boarding the plane I saw that the pilot was black. I had never seen a black pilot before, and the instant I did I had to quell my panic. How could a black man fly a plane? But a moment later I caught myself: I had fallen into the apartheid mind-set, thinking that Africans were inferior and that flying was a white man's job. (Mandela, 1994: 347–8)

Nelson Mandela is of course a very confident, very able and very assertive man, who kept faith with his political beliefs and his opposition to white minority rule, in spite of 25 years in prison. But, though he had spent his life fighting the kind of racist attitude that said that black people could not do skilled, responsible jobs like flying airliners, even he had internalised a bit of that attitude himself. The term 'internalised oppression' refers exactly to this kind of process, whereby the oppressed take on and adopt the oppressor's stereotypes. As Freire writes:

> Self-deprecation is another characteristic of the oppressed, which derives from their internalisation of the opinion that oppressors hold of them. So often do they hear that they are good for nothing, know nothing and are incapable of learning anything – that they are sick, lazy and unproductive – that in the end they become convinced of their own unfitness. (Freire, 1993: 45)

The negative labels that others apply to people can have a surprisingly direct, and often unconscious, effect on how we see ourselves and how we act. Becca Levy describes a number of psychological experiments with old people, in which either 'positive age-stereotype words (e.g. wisdom) or negative age-stereotype words (e.g. decrepit) were flashed on a computer screen at speeds designed to allow perception without awareness' (2003: 206). Those who were exposed to the negative words – and remember their exposure to the words was so rapid that they themselves were not even conscious of having seen them – performed less well on memory tasks and even *walked* more slowly than those exposed to the positive words. If even brief exposure to words has this effect, it is quite frightening to think of the potential effect of the labels that social workers and other professionals routinely apply, not only to old people, but to most of the people they work with.

Another insidious way in which social workers can unintentionally feed into the internalised oppression of service users is by encouraging dependency. A person who feels useless can easily be persuaded that it is better to hand over all his problems to someone else to solve, and a social worker who, for whatever reason, is willing to take on a service user's problems, as opposed to supporting the service user in resolving them for himself, is in danger of entrenching this pattern. (If someone says 'Do this for me, I can't do it myself', and you do it, then you are really confirming that they indeed can't do it for themselves.) Social workers may be particularly vulnerable to making this kind of mistake when they feel a bit useless themselves, and therefore long for praise and approval. It is something to watch out for when you start out.

OPPRESSION, OBJECTIFICATION AND 'RESPECT FOR PERSONS'

When Israel was in Egypt's land

Let my people go

Oppressed so hard they could not stand

Let my people go ...

(African-American spiritual)

There are two aspects to oppression: the structural fact and the subjective experience. On the one hand, the word 'oppression' refers to an unequal power relationship which is abused or misused in the interest of the powerful. On the other hand, 'oppression' refers to the individual experience of being weighed down and crushed. To understand how oppression works, we need to understand how power operates in society. To understand why oppression *matters*, we need to understand what it does to human beings.

What, in human terms (as opposed to structural ones), do oppressors do to those they oppress? They crush their spirits, they deny them their rights, and deny them their humanity. You will remember that, in Kant's philosophy, discussed in Chapter 2, what underlay the idea of respect for persons was the 'categorical imperative': people are ends in themselves, not means to an end. Oppression involves ignoring this fact.

Perhaps the ultimate case of treating people as means rather than ends is that of slavery, for a slave is treated as an object, a possession to be bought, sold and used for whatever purpose is convenient. Slavery epitomises the process of *objectifying* human beings that is characteristic, to a greater or lesser extent, of all forms of oppression.

Objectification

Treating a human being not as a 'subject' (an autonomous being capable of acting in her own right) but as an 'object'. Literally means 'turning into an object'.

Horne (1999: 82–3) argues that one of the most basic functions of ethical social work is to 'create the subject' by, so to speak, finding the human being behind the objectifying label ('mental patient', 'delinquent', 'schizophrenic'...).

The word 'othering' (Dominelli, 2002: 18) is also quite often used, to describe the process whereby we set someone at a distance from ourselves by defining them as 'other'.

We might think that slavery was a thing of the past, but unfortunately it is still very much with us: 'The ILO estimates that a minimum of 12.3 million people are enslaved in the world today. These include at least 360,000 in industrialised countries, of which at least 270,000 have been trafficked into forced labour' (Craig et al., 2007: 20).

Slavery is, however, an extreme case. Oppression occurs all around us in more insidious, less obvious ways. Indeed, we can easily find instances of objectification of human beings not only within society at large but within social work itself. It occurs when social worker and social work agencies act as the instrument of policies that have the effect of 'objectifying' people, and it occurs when social workers and social work agencies 'objectify' human beings to meet their own personal or organisational needs.

The latter can occur in a number of ways and for a number of reasons. When working a great deal with human suffering, it is natural and human to want to defend yourself against being overwhelmed by it. When required to do difficult things that will distress people – removing a child from a parent, insisting that an elderly person leave her home – it is necessary to defend oneself against one's own feelings of distress and guilt, and you will find this is so, even if you are sure the action is justified. One way of managing those negative feelings is to stop seeing the service user as a fellow human being and to start seeing them just as a 'service user' or a 'client', a member, so to speak, of a different species, whose suffering is somehow not as real as our own. It is particularly easy to do this if the service user belongs to a different group from yourself: a different class, a different ethnic group, a different age group … .

In fact, if you look just at the language that is used in social work offices, it is often steeped in terminology that has the effect of objectifying people. Consider the term 'bed blocker' (used to describe patients, usually elderly, who are seen as in need of prompt removal from hospital so as to free up beds). Or the simple word 'case'. Or the use of the word 'intake' to describe a team that deal with new refer- rals, rather as if human needs could be processed like some kind of industrial mate- rial being sucked into a machine. Anne Wilson and Peter Beresford (2000) criticise anti-oppressive practice as it is written and talked about in academic social work, for focusing on oppression based on race, gender and class, and yet not recognising just *being a service user* as a form of difference or a category of social division' in its own right (2000: 563, original emphasis). 'Yet,' they go on to say, 'it is frequently if not generally experienced as one, with its own issues of power inequality, dis- crimination and oppression' (2000: 563). It is a very important point. Recognising oppression is not just a question of counting up 'isms' (such as racism and sexism, of which there will be more in Chapter 11). There is huge potential for social work agencies to be oppressive towards service users per se, regardless of their gender, class or ethnicity. A useful exercise when you are on placement is to notice the ways in which social workers distance themselves from service users by using language that objectifies them, or reduces them to problems rather than people.

It *is* necessary in social work, for the sake of your own mental health, to find ways of protecting yourself from the distress that often surrounds you – we do need defences – but this means that it is important to find other ways of looking after yourself that do not involve stopping treating people as people and starting treating them as objects. (This is probably particularly easy in respect of people who are not in a position to insist on their own viewpoint being heard, such as small children, but it can happen with service users of all ages.)

A simple test, then, that can be used to help answer the question 'Am I acting oppressively?' is: 'Am I treating people with respect: as ends in themselves and not just means?'

OPPRESSION AND DISCRIMINATION

We have already noted that the term 'anti-oppressive' is used so frequently in the social work literature as to run the risk that we may stop thinking about what it is supposed to mean. The same applies to the word 'anti-discriminatory'. In fact, to make things more difficult, the latter is sometimes used interchangeably with 'anti-oppressive' and at other times as if there was a clear distinction between the two. (It does not reflect particularly well on the general standard of discourse in social work education, that we have been more insistent on the use of these terms than we have been interested in being consistent about what we mean by them.) Thus, on the one hand, Neil Thompson writes, in his well-known book on anti-discriminatory practice, that 'anti-discriminatory and anti-oppressive practice are … presented here as more or less synonymous' (2006: xii). Jane Dalrymple and Beverley Burke, however, see them as quite distinct, taking the view that an anti-discriminatory approach, which they see as challenging discrimination through legal means, is narrower, and 'limiting in its potential to challenge oppression' (2006: 4).

However, although the words 'oppression' and 'discrimination' certainly mean different things, the two are closely linked in practice. First, to discriminate against someone without a valid reason is often oppressive in effect. (Banks [2006: 15] gives an example of travellers excluded from a playgroup on the grounds that their presence would upset other parents.) Second, as Thompson says, 'discrimination is the process (or set of processes) that leads to oppression' (2006: xii). It is social divisions (such as class, gender or ethnicity) that 'form the basis of the social structure … which plays such an important role in the distribution of power, status and opportunities' (2006: 21). In other words, for one group to be oppressed, that group has first to be defined as *different*.

The following historical example may help to illustrate this. As we mentioned in Chapter 2, the USA was founded on the idea that it was a 'self-evident' truth that every man had the right to 'life, liberty and the pursuit of happiness'. How then did this nation, of all nations, manage to justify the abduction of millions of human beings from Africa to be bought and sold like cattle in the 'Land of the Free'? The answer is that it was done (in the USA, but also by the British, who used slaves in Caribbean colonies such as Jamaica, Guyana and Barbados) by discriminating so sharply between people on the grounds of their skin colour, that black people could be treated as if they were not fully human. A similar process allowed the Nazis to exterminate millions of Jews and gypsies in the gas chambers on the grounds that they were 'subhuman'. The same kind of discrimination, on grounds of 'race', was used to justify the colonial annexation, by Britain, France and other European powers, of countries already inhabited by dark-skinned people.

Slavery was only made illegal in 1833 in the British Empire and in 1865 in the USA. (It may seem a long time ago, but there are elderly people still alive today in the USA, Britain and the West Indies who in their childhood would have met old people who had been born into legal slavery.) Colonial rule by Britain of dozens of African, Asian and Caribbean countries ended much more recently, within the memory of the authors of this book, as did legal segregation of black and white in the southern states of America. South African apartheid, which perpetuated the rigid, legally sanctioned hierarchy of white over black that was normal in the British Empire, was dismantled only 20 years or so before the publication of this edition.

We have given the above account of the historic origins of racism, though, not just for its own sake, but because it is a good example of the way that discrimination can be used to justify oppression. It is important to remind ourselves how recent this history is because it helps us to understand why racism is very much still with us and in us, both as individuals and as a society, and why as social workers it is essential to take seriously the everyday reality of racism by black and Asian people. However, it is possible to think of examples which are more recent and closer to home, of the ways in which discriminatory thinking can be used to justify oppression.

EXERCISE 9.3

OPPRESSION JUSTIFIED BY DISCRIMINATORY THINKING

Can you think of examples that you might encounter in social work or social care, now or in the past, of situations in which oppressive behaviour was justified or rationalised by discriminatory thinking?

Comments on Exercise 9.3

Here are a few suggestions:

- Adults with learning disabilities are denied control over their own finances, denied the right to form sexual relationships, or to have privacy in their living accommodation on the grounds that 'they are really just like children'. (One of the authors of this book – Chris – started his working life as a nursing auxiliary in an institution where middle-aged men who were more than able enough to read and write were routinely referred to as 'boys' and slept in dormitories with only a small bedside cupboard to keep their personal belongings in.)
- The absence of service users from ethnic minorities on the caseload of an adult assessment team is justified on the grounds that 'they look after their own'.
- A violent assault on a child is tolerated because 'it is normal in their culture'.

People who behave in oppressive ways have to justify to themselves the fact that they are treating a group of people differently from how they would like to be treated themselves. This is much easier to do if they can persuade themselves that these other people are somehow inferior to themselves. Both on a very small scale, and on the very large societal scale that justifies slavery and empire and genocide, the same dynamic is at work. Figure 9.1 illustrates this oppressive cycle at work and suggests a number of points at which, even if only in small ways, social workers can try to challenge and interrupt it.

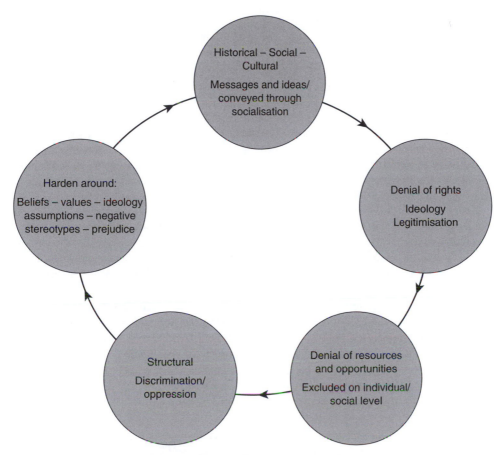

Figure 9.1   The cycle of oppression and discrimination

'MINIMAL INTERVENTION'

We will conclude this chapter by drawing your attention to a simple but crucial aspect of 'anti-oppressive' practice which we have borrowed from Jane Dalrymple and Beverley Burke (2006): the principle of *minimal intervention*.

Any social work intervention is an intrusion, however well meant, into the privacy of an individual's or a family's life. Most social workers are acting as agents of the state, which means that (whether they like it or not) their encounters with service users are based on a gigantic power imbalance. All social workers represent, and have the backing of, organisations, so that even in the non-statutory sector the power imbalance is still very much present. Dalrymple and Burke go so far as to say that the word intervention 'by its very nature indicates where the dominant power relations are situated' (2006: 159). (Simply changing the word, though, would of course not alter the fact.)

It is therefore important for social workers not to think of intervention as necessarily a 'good thing', even if well meant. On the contrary, it is something to be avoided unless (a) it is clearly requested by the service user and/or is clearly required for the protection of others who are not in a position to protect themselves, and (b) there are strong indications that it would be helpful. Simply to intervene in order to prove that you 'tried to do something' is not good practice.

If intervention is necessary, then there remain many ways in which social workers can, if not eliminate, at least reduce the sense of intervention as being something 'done to' a service user and make it into something which is 'done with', 'on behalf of' or 'in consultation with' the service user (even if not truly done 'in partnership', which implies an equal power relationship). Here are a few suggestions:

- being clear why you are involved, and what are the rules, limits and timescale of your involvement;
- explaining to service users how you record your work with them and providing them with copies of your records (or jointly discussing how your meetings with them are to be recorded);
- not consulting other professionals about the service user, or passing on information to others about the service user, without the service user's permission and knowledge (or in situations where it really has to be done anyway, at least informing the service user in advance about the nature and extent of information sharing that will go on);
- inviting the service user to give his or her own explanations of what is going on in her life and being extremely wary of offering your own explanations;
- asking service users how they wish to be addressed, and not simply calling people by their first names;
- being clear and honest about the purpose of your involvement and not using devious means to 'make things easier' for the service user or yourself (i.e. if you are visiting to check up on them, say so; do not pretend you are there for some other purpose);
- not using jargon, or explaining it properly if you have to use it.

All of these points really add up to treating service users as we would expect to be treated by professionals: with respect.

CHAPTER SUMMARY

This chapter has tried to revive the overused word 'oppression', and demonstrate the importance of the idea for social work. We have suggested that oppression is the opposite of respect, but oppression has a structural component as well as a purely personal one. It affects whole groups, not just individuals, and among those groups, are not only people who are discriminated against because of their ethnicity, gender, class or disability, but people who are negatively labelled simply for being social work service users.

We have discussed the internalisation of oppression, the way that people who are being oppressed will often take on board the negative evaluations of themselves that they receive from their oppressors. We have also discussed the process of 'othering' or 'objectification' which prepares the ground for oppression, and we have noted that this can easily occur within social work, and not just in the world outside. We have also discussed the relationship between 'oppression' and 'discrimination', and concluded with a discussion of the principle of 'minimal intervention', a phrase we borrowed from Dalrymple and Burke (2006).

 # FURTHER READING

Two useful recent books which we have discussed in this chapter and would commend to the reader are:

Clifford, D. and Burke, B. (2009) *Anti-oppressive Ethics and Values in Social Work.* Basingstoke: Palgrave.

Dalrymple, J. and Burke, B. (2006) *Anti-oppressive Practice: Social Care and the Law*, 2nd edn. Maidenhead: McGraw Hill.

10

ETHICS AND RESOURCES

- Practitioners and managers
- Different philosophies
- Who should decide?
- Equity or advocacy?
- Working within limits
- Challenging shortfalls

The American political scientist Russell Hardin commented that the US code of social work ethics, like that of medicine, fails the professionals it is supposed to serve because it 'neglects the greatest range of actual cases of difficult moral choices they will face on the job' (1990: 540). New professionals, he went on to say, will find as a result that, not only are they 'unable to fulfil the grandiose principles of their ethical codes, but they will typically have no categories to apply to the difficult moral choices they have to make' (1990: 540).

The particular difficult choices he is referring to result from the fact that the resources available to social workers to carry out any given task are determined by others, even though 'it is the social worker ... who faces the burden of saying no when a needed service ... is contrary to policy' (1990: 538), and it is the welfare professions too who, 'in addition to their direct concern with welfare ... must be concerned with the fairness of their services and with making reasonable trade-offs between competing, honorable ends' (1990: 539). If we only have a limited amount of time and money, how should we best use it?

Actually, the British Association of Social Workers' Code of Ethics does make mention of resources when it says that 'Social workers should ensure that resources at their disposal are distributed fairly, according to need' (BASW, 2012: 9), but Hardin is probably right in saying that these kinds of exhortations do not always help us very much when we have more referrals coming in than we can allocate, or when we know that, in order to offer a service to one client, we must necessarily deny it to another.

Indeed, it is not just the case that our codes of ethics have very little to say about this, for literature on social work, and even policy guidance, are surprisingly silent on these matters. There is a literature in health care about the ethical principles behind the distribution of limited resources (see, for example, Daniels and Sabin, 2008), but there is remarkably little in social work, with some authors of social work texts even seeming to think that social workers should not, as it were, sully their hands with such decisions at all. (Lena Dominelli, for instance, disapproves of resources being made 'available only for those groups that have been specifically targeted as needing them' [2002: 27], and of 'narrowly defined criteria of eligibility' [2002: 36].) This seems rather unhelpful, given that many, if not most, student social workers will soon be working in posts whose very job descriptions implicate them in such decisions. Indeed, one of the main uses to which social work assessments are put is to provide information on which decisions about resource allocation are made. Even if we leave that aside, the fact remains that each individual social worker has to make decisions about how to distribute the resources represented by her own time. As they move into management positions, social workers do not necessarily turn into the heartless bureaucrats so beloved of TV hospital soaps, but they do start having to think, not just about how to distribute their own time, but about the time of all the staff who answer to them.

When this is the reality, it seems right that a book on social work ethics should deal with the ethics of resource allocation, even if many commentators on social work prefer not to discuss this. To paraphrase a point Chris Beckett has made previously (Beckett, 2007, 2010; Walker and Beckett, 2010), social work academics, journalists, politicians and public figures can, if they wish, decline to engage with the fact that there are only so many hours in the day, but social work practitioners and social work managers have no choice but to take this into account. Indeed, although we might feel that social work and social care ought to have more resources at its disposal than it actually does (and we are writing at a time when cuts in social work services, and other parts of the public sector, are being made to repay debts caused by catastrophic failures in the banking industry), it is hard to conceive of a system where *some* decisions did not have to be made about how to allocate resources. Writing about health care, Daniels and Sabin point out:

> even a wealthy country with a highly efficient health care system will have to set limits to – in other words, ration – the health care it guarantees everyone. However important, health care ... is not the only important social good. Societies must also provide education, jobs, transportation, energy, defense, research, art and culture ... Society simply cannot meet all medical needs, and certainly not all medical preferences, so it must decide which needs should be given priority and when resources are better spent elsewhere. (2008: 2)

The same is surely true of social work and social care.

PRESSURE ON YOUR WORKLOAD

You are a childcare social worker in the statutory sector. Your special interest is working with children in the public care system who require placement in substitute families, but who are recognised as being 'hard to place'. You are working intensively with several such children, helping to prepare them for placement and to prepare foster families for their difficult task. It is generally accepted that to do this work successfully requires skill and a good deal of time. Up to now, your caseload has been protected in recognition of this fact, and in recognition of the fact that inadequate preparation will result in an increased likelihood of placement breakdown (which would be difficult for the agency and, of course, disastrous for the children). You have had a caseload of eight such children at any one time.

However, staff shortages in the agency and an influx of child protection referrals have created a problem. Your manager says he has no choice but to ask you to take on some of these new child protection cases, over and above your existing caseload. This will involve you in joint investigations, attendance at child protection conferences and possibly court work.

How do you respond?

Comments on Exercise 10.1

We don't think there is an easy answer to this. The work you are already doing is difficult and time-consuming and very important, but so is the work that the manager is seeking to allocate. What is clear is that there is no possibility that you could take on this new work and carry on delivering the same quality of service to the children on your existing caseload.

Your agency has a responsibility to protect children who seem to be at risk, but it also holds a parental responsibility for children in public care. Our suggestion is that when social workers are placed in a position where they know they are unable to discharge their agency's legal responsibilities to vulnerable people (in this case children), they should ensure that steps are taken to inform those with overall responsibility for the service – including elected politicians – about the shortfall, making absolutely clear that, if task B is to be taken on, task A will not be properly carried out. We cannot necessarily determine what resources are placed at our disposal, or what jobs we are asked to do, but we can insist on stating what will and will not be possible with the resources available.

PRACTITIONERS AND MANAGERS

In social work agencies, there is typically a division of responsibility in which social work practitioners assess needs, but managers, themselves usually social workers by training, make decisions about how resources should be allocated. As one of us has observed elsewhere (Walker and Beckett, 2010: 75), this arrangement has some psychological advantages for all concerned. Front-line practitioners can blame their managers for not making resources available to service users ('They don't care, all they think about is money!'). Managers in turn can dissociate themselves from the day-to-day contact with human distress and distance themselves from responsibility for any casework that goes wrong.

We should not assume, though, that this split of responsibilities is necessarily the most healthy way of running a social work agency. (McCaffrey [1998] suggests that it is an instance of the defence mechanism known in the psychoanalytic literature as 'splitting'.) Perhaps resources would be better distributed if practitioners themselves were responsible for budgets? Hudson and Henwood (2008: 27) make a distinction between 'rationing by directive', which is more likely to occur when resource decisions are made in a top-down way based on rules and procedures, and 'managing by discretion', which is what can occur when budgetary decisions are devolved to practitioners. (They also note, incidentally [2008: 34], that there is a different mix between these two approaches in adult social care, from that which exists in children's social care.)

However these decisions are taken in an agency, we should certainly be under no illusions, whether we are managers or practitioners, that leaving it to others to make difficult decisions somehow entitles us to take the moral high ground. A social worker who collects information that a manager will use to make decisions about priorities is morally implicated in those decisions. Likewise, a manager who gives a social worker a piece of work to do, and inadequate resources to do it with, must share responsibility for the success or failure of that piece of work. (The inquiry into the death of Victoria Climbié rightly criticised senior managers for attempting to distance themselves from responsibility for the tragedy by saying that they were not responsible for the 'day-to-day realities' [Laming, 2003: 5].)

Psychological splitting does have the benefit to both front-line staff and managers of reducing anxiety – sharing out the pain – but too rigid a split between 'practice' decisions and 'resource' decisions ignores the fact that the two types of decision are closely intertwined. In reality, at *every* level of a social work agency, from practitioner to director, staff have to think not only about what it would be desirable to do in an ideal world, but also about what it is possible to do in the world *as it actually is*. (This is the 'duty of realism' that we discussed in Chapter 5.) This involves making choices about who gets a service at any given moment and who does not. Even just in deciding how to divide up her time, a social worker is involved in making this type of decision, as the following exercise illustrates:

THE GREENS' FINANCIAL PROBLEMS

You are working with the Green family on a variety of problems. You are aware that their problems are exacerbated by a lack of money. In particular, the family could really do with a washing machine (one of the children wets the bed) but cannot afford one. The benefits

EXERCISE 10.2

(Cont'd)

system (for whatever reason) cannot help. Your own agency is also unable to provide the necessary funds. Your manager says that this simply cannot be regarded as a high enough priority for a payment to be made out of the agency's small budget for one-off grants. However, a colleague tells you that you should be able to raise enough money by applying to charities. Your colleague tells you that the trick is not to ask any one charity for too large a grant but to make multiple applications to different charities asking for small contributions.

This looks like a time-consuming task. It will mean seeking out appropriate charities, finding out the application process in each case (which will often involve writing or telephoning to obtain application forms) and completing a series of applications, each in a slightly different format.

Many of the other families you work with also have financial problems, but you could not possibly commit this amount of time to obtaining funds from charities for each of them.

The time spent on applying to charities for the Greens will also be time taken from other work. For instance, you are behind on your visits to children in foster homes.

How will you decide whether or not you can justify spending time on applying to charities to pay for a washing machine for the Greens?

Comments on Exercise 10.2

You may have concluded that to make a decision about this you need to decide how serious the consequences would be for the Green family of continuing to struggle on without a washing machine, and compare this with the possible consequences of putting off or not doing the other things that you might have done with the time. This would be a utilitarian approach. (Refer back to Chapter 2 if you need to remind yourself of the difference between utilitarian and deontological approaches.) Given that you don't necessarily know the consequences of different courses of action, it would be hard to apply consistently.

On the other hand, you may have concluded that, if the Greens are eligible for financial help from a charity, then it is your duty to ensure that they get it, regardless of the time it takes you. This would be a more deontological stance. (Again, see Chapter 2 if you are not clear what this means. The difficulty with it is, of course, that there are only so many hours in your week.)

The main point we wish to make with this exercise, though, is simply that even an individual social worker, considering how to deal with her own caseload, is involved in decision making about the deployment of resources which is no different in principle from the kinds of decision about resources that are made by senior managers or politicians.

DIFFERENT PHILOSOPHIES

What are the ethical principles involved in deciding how time and other resources are allocated? Should resources be spread as widely as possible, or should they be targeted? If they *are* targeted, should this be done on the basis of those whose needs are greatest, or (and this is not necessarily the same thing) on the basis of those who would benefit the most? Should they be concentrated on helping those in crisis, or should they be spent on reducing the number of situations that reach crisis point in the first place? As Cookson et al. observe, there is a tension 'between the injunction to do as much good as possible with scarce resources and the injunction to rescue identifiable individuals in immediate peril, regardless of cost' (2008: 540).

The article just cited actually relates to health rather than social care, and, to date, most of the academic discussion of these kinds of question does seem to take place in the health field. There is a substantial literature in health addressing such questions as the use of numerical 'quality of life' measures to determine priorities (Ovretveit, 1998), the admissibility of taking the personal characteristics of patients into account when deciding how to allocate resources (Olsen et al., 2003) and the philosophical ideas underpinning resource allocation. Thus, Girling (1993) suggested that, in a medical context, 'clinicians' ('practitioners' in social work terms) and their managers typically start from different philosophical bases when approaching these kinds of decision. Managers tend to adopt a utilitarian stance, Girling suggests, while clinicians are more comfortable with a deontological approach, which 'may incidentally account for the apparent fact that managers and clinicians sometimes seem to inhabit different ethical universes' (Girling, 1993: 41–2).

This observation about the philosophical gulf between managers and practitioners is relevant to social work agencies as well as to health services (even though in British social work, unlike in health care, most managers are themselves qualified practitioners). A social work manager who turns down a request from a social worker for funding on the grounds that other cases have higher priority may feel she is sincerely doing her best, in true utilitarian style, to deploy limited resources to the maximum possible effect. However, the social worker may see the decision as a failure to recognise her service user's right to a better life and the agency's duty to provide it.

We do not propose to try to set down here which is the 'right' philosophical approach to such decisions. We discussed in Chapter 2 the merits and shortcomings of both deontological and utilitarian approaches, but you may like to consider for yourself how you would deal with the situation described in the following exercise.

MR BROWN OR MR REES?

You are a social worker in a team whose task is to assess the care needs of elderly people. If you conclude that residential care is needed, the way that your particular agency operates is that you have to present the case for your client at a weekly panel, chaired by a senior manager. Funds for residential beds are limited, and the job of the panel is to decide who needs it most.

EXERCISE 10.3

(Cont'd)

One week you have two cases to present to the panel, both involving elderly men who feel they need residential care. It happens that, in this particular week, no other cases are being presented, but the panel can only fund one residential bed.

You present the case as fairly as possible, for each of your clients (some details are given below), but the panel admits that it finds it difficult to decide between the two. After some discussion, the chair of the panel asks you for your help.

'Both of these cases seem equally high priority to us,' the chair says. 'But you know these two men. Which of the two does your gut instinct tell us we should help first?'

How do you respond?

Mr Brown

Aged 84, Mr Brown lives alone and has little in the way of extended family support. He is physically frail and has had a number of nasty falls requiring hospital treatment. He already receives a high level of homecare support, but it is not 24-hour and Mr Brown lives in fear of falling and hurting himself and not being able to get help.

Mr Rees

Aged 84, Mr Rees lives with his wife, aged 79, who is his main carer. He is physically frail and has had a number of nasty falls. Mr Rees and his wife have a very unhappy relationship. She resents having to care for him and there are some indications that the stress of it is taking a toll on her own health. Although you cannot prove it, you have a strong suspicion that Mrs Rees may be taking out her frustrations on Mr Rees himself. He seems frightened in her presence – even sometimes flinches when she comes near him – and, though he makes no complaints about her, is very anxious to move to residential care.

Comments on Exercise 10.3

One way of responding would be to say something like this:

> 'I'm sorry but I don't think that it is up to me to choose between the two. I think both these men need residential care. I have promised both of them I will do my best to obtain it for them and I have presented their cases as fairly as I can. I feel that I should leave the decision to the panel as to which of these men will lose out.'

In some circumstances, such a position might be the best one to take. However, in practice the choice will still be made and, if you are not prepared to participate in it, the panel – who do not know anything about either Mr Brown or Mr Rees other than what you have included in your report – will make it on their own. Perhaps, if you do have any sense that one of these cases should be a higher priority than the other, you ought to share your views with the panel.

If so, you would need to find some way of weighing up, for instance, the greater risk to Mr Brown of falling and lying undiscovered for some time, as against the possibly greater risk to Mr Rees of being physically abused. You might do this by thinking in terms of absolute rights ('all elderly people are entitled to be protected against physical abuse', for instance) or you might adopt the approach of trying to compare the amount of suffering caused to each man in his present circumstances, or trying to compare the risks. The former approach is more 'deontological', the latter 'utilitarian', to refer once again to the philosophical positions we discussed in Chapter 2.

WHO SHOULD DECIDE?

We have already discussed the division of responsibilities for decisions about resources between social work managers and social work practitioners, but of course there are more potential decision makers than just these two groups, not least the users of social work services themselves. Given that the total 'pot' of money available to run a given service is made at a political level (of which more about later), there are actually a number of different ways in which decisions might be made as to how the service should best deploy that budget. And here too, there are ethical questions as well as merely practical ones. (Who *ought* to be making these decisions?)

Hudson and Henwood identify 'five different approaches to resource allocation used in social care, each one with a different underpinning rationale' (2008: 30). We list them here using their terminology, but with our own summaries:

- *Professional discretion.* Rationing is 'implicit', rather than being based on published eligibility criteria, on the basis that professionals are 'best placed to exercise informed judgement' (2008: 30).
- *Service-led criteria.* Rationing is carried out by setting criteria for access to specific services. Thus, there are specific criteria set for admission to, say, a day centre, or for access to domiciliary care. This is an approach which was supposed to have been set aside by the 1990 NHS and Community Care Act, with its emphasis on 'needs-led' rather than 'service-led' assessment.
- *Needs and risks criteria.* A hierarchy of needs and risks is used to determine eligibility. Government guidance for adult social care, for example, sets out four levels of eligibility based on need and risk: 'critical', 'substantial', 'moderate' and 'low' (DoH, 2010).
- *Outcome-based criteria.* Here, rather than base eligibility on needs and risks, it is based on the outcomes likely to be achieved, such as the five outcomes on which the UK government's *Every Child Matters* programme is based (DfE, 2008).
- *User/carer discretion.* Direct payments to service users place the service user and carer in charge of deciding what services they need most, and would prefer. However, it is important to note that the actual size of the payment made remains subject to the control of state agencies. 'The right to self-determination will be at the heart of a reformed system,'

says *Putting People First* (DoH, 2007: 2), 'only constrained by the realities of finite resources and levels of protection, which should be responsible but not risk averse'. The deployment of resources is therefore devolved to service users, but the allocation of them remains the responsibility of the state, to be decided by one or other of the four previous approaches. A more truly user/care-led approach to resource allocation would be occurring if, for instance, a 'pot' of money was made available to a user/carer-run organisation, for it to distribute to its members as they thought fit.

We will not attempt to decide here which of these methods is the best, but you may like to ask yourself which system you would favour yourself, whether as a social worker, or a service user. Is your answer the same in either case?

EQUITY OR ADVOCACY?

We have been discussing how resources should be distributed, or, to speak more bluntly, how they should be *rationed*. Rationing in some form is inevitable. Given that any social work service has limited resources – a residential unit has only so many beds, a fieldwork team has only so many hours of social worker time, a day-care facility has a limit to the number of people it can take in – it is only ever possible to provide a service to one person at the cost of reducing the amount of services that are available to others. This can place individual social workers in a difficult ethical position. Should she first and foremost be an advocate for her own client, presenting the client's case in as convincing a way as possible, so as to maximise the chances of the client obtaining the desired service? Or, alternatively, should her primary obligation be to contribute to the agency's efforts to distribute its resources as fairly and consistently as possible, in which case the social worker might have to concede at times that her client's need was not as great as the need of others? (Exercise 10.3 highlighted this dilemma by posing a situation where a social worker was asked to choose between two of her clients.)

This is yet another instance where two ethical principles pull us in different directions. On the one hand, there is the principle of wholehearted commitment to one's service users, on the other hand the principle of fairness or equity.

To complicate matters still further, there is a danger that in advocating too rigorously on behalf of a particular service user, a social worker may actually do that individual service user a disservice by emphasising his level of need and/or the degree to which he is at risk, and thereby *labelling* him, in a way that may cause that service user problems in the future. An example of this would be if a social worker emphasised, or exaggerated, the level of risk to children in a family in order to get access for that family to resources which were only available to high-risk cases. This might be helpful to the family in the sense that it might indeed result in those resources being made available, but it could also result in the family being given a 'child protection' label, which might colour their dealings with professional agencies for many years to come.

WORKING WITHIN LIMITS

In social work, as in other areas of life, there are many interventions which may be highly beneficial and desirable if undertaken properly, but which are better not attempted at all if they are not adequately resourced. As we discussed earlier in Chapter 5, a decision as to whether or not a given course of action is appropriate therefore often depends in part on whether or not the resources – money, time or expertise – are available to carry it out properly. The duty of realism (as we called it in Chapter 5) requires that a responsible social worker pay due attention to these considerations before embarking on a piece of work. This is very obvious if we think about contexts other than social work. Imagine, for instance, that the slates on the roof of your house were getting old and the roof was beginning to leak. It might be desirable to replace them, but you would certainly not consider removing them unless you had first ensured that you had the funds to pay for new ones. A leaky roof, after all, is a lot better than no roof at all.

In a social work context, though, we have sometimes heard it argued that, if a given course of action is desirable, it should be carried out *regardless of resource considerations*. This is the equivalent of removing the roof of a house without first ensuring that it will be possible to replace it, except that what is at stake in a social work decision is not just the fabric of a building but the well-being, and even the entire life course, of a human being. To embark on a course of action without ensuring that it can be properly carried through is not just foolhardy, but irresponsible. It would be irresponsible, for instance, for a social work agency to remove a child from his family, without being reasonably confident that it will be able to meet the child's needs better than the family could.

Likewise, it would be irresponsible for a social worker to embark on a programme of in-depth therapeutic work with a service user if she did not have the time to carry it through properly, or if adequate support was not available for the service user in the event of him being distressed by the issues that came up in the course of the work.

CHALLENGING SHORTFALLS

Some readers might raise an objection to what we have been saying in the chapter so far.

'You seem to be arguing,' they might exclaim, 'that we should collude with the system in rationing out resources and cutting back services to people who need them. You seem to be arguing that we should simply accept the world as it is. Surely we should be challenging the system when it is inadequately resourced, and fighting on behalf of service users to get the services to which they are entitled?'

Let us be quite clear, therefore, that an important part of the 'duty of realism' in relation to resources is that social workers *should* challenge inadequate provision by their agencies, and by society, rather than collude in the pretence that unrealistic objectives are actually attainable without appropriate resources. Our point is that to attempt to take on impossible tasks is not the right way for either individuals or social work agencies to challenge the existing system. On the contrary, it serves to bolster up inadequate provision, by creating an unrealistic impression of what a service is really able to achieve. An example of this is provided by Broadhurst et al. (2010), in their study of initial assessments carried out by social workers of child and family cases. They describe busy social workers attempting to meet deadlines for the completion of assessments by cutting corners: leaving parts of the assessment uncompleted, for instance, or signing off the assessment when important information was still missing. The behaviour of these social workers is understandable, given the pressure on them and their managers to complete assessments on time and so allow their local authorities to meet performance targets, but it is not really helpful. By sacrificing quality and accuracy to meet their deadlines, they were giving the *impression* that they were doing the job assigned to them with the resources available – they were, one might say, allowing their agencies to tick the required boxes – but it was a *false* impression. In fact, they were placing service users, and their own professional reputations, at risk.

Much of the public policy that social workers are required to implement – and much of the public criticism of social work that regularly takes place – does not fully pass what we might call the 'reality test'. Social workers are regularly asked to carry out tasks which are simply not possible with the resources available. One of us has argued previously, for instance (Beckett, 2010: 16), that it was unreasonable of Lord Laming, in his report on the Victoria Climbié tragedy, to criticise social services departments for 'devising ways of limiting access to services, and adopting mechanisms to reduce service demand' (Laming, 2003: 11), particularly as he also, in the same report, insisted that no case be allocated to a social worker unless he or she has 'the time to deal with it properly' (2003: 337). Since they have limited resources and since their staff are not superhuman or in possession of time machines, social services departments quite obviously have *no choice* but to limit access to services, if they are to protect their staff against impossible caseloads. They can only hope to do so as fairly and as transparently as possible.

The need to ration limited resources often results in social workers having to act in ways that go directly against the instincts which led them into social work in the first place – we are assuming that no one becomes a social worker in order to refuse services to people in need – but it is no solution at all to pretend to be fulfilling duties which in practice it is impossible to meet. Far from 'challenging the system', attempting to do the impossible, or pretending to be doing more than you can really do, in fact lets the system 'off the hook', creates a false impression that needs are being met when they are not, and allows blame to be pinned unjustly to individual social workers, or social work agencies, for the problems that inevitably arise. Part of the duty of realism is to publicly state when resources are inadequate to the task, by being honest about the duties that are not being properly discharged and the risks that are being taken. This is clearly implied in the British Association of Social Worker's Code of Ethics, which requires social workers to:

> bring to the attention of their employers, policy makers, politicians and the general public situations where resources are inadequate or where distribution of resources, policies and practice are oppressive, unfair, harmful or illegal. (BASW, 2012: 9)

You may remember a social worker, quoted by Ferguson and Woodward, who we discussed in Chapter 4. 'Unwilling to turn a blind eye to unmet need and service user distress', she 'almost constantly "passed information back up the line to senior managers"' (2009: 158). A recent example in the news of an employee flagging up resource shortcomings in this way, comes, not from social work, but from the railway industry. At the inquest into the death of Margaret Masson, an elderly woman who died in a train crash at Grayrigg in Cumbria in 2007, it was established that the accident had been caused by a faulty set of points, resulting in the train coming off the rails and running down an embankment. David Lewis, an engineer with Network Rail, broke down in tears at the hearing when he admitted that he had forgotten to check the points in question. However, it emerged that Mr Lewis had repeatedly warned the company that shortage of staff was making it impossible to check the lines thoroughly, and was placing rail users at risk. Mrs Masson's son commented: 'Before I knew anything about this, I wanted to take [Mr Lewis'] head off his shoulders ... Now I totally respect him. He's got my utmost respect for what he tried to do...' (BBC News, 2011b: online). No doubt Mr Lewis will still always reproach himself for the death of Mrs Masson and the injuries caused to 88 others, but there must be some comfort to him in knowing that he had tried to warn the company that this might happen, and in having had these efforts recognised and applauded by Mrs Masson's own family.

IMPOSSIBLE DEMANDS

EXERCISE 10.4

Gill works in a children and families social work team. She is required to complete assessments within a short timeframe, and pressure of work means that she can only do this by cutting corners, as discussed above, and by getting assessments signed off as completed, when in fact they are missing important information. Her manager is under pressure to increase the percentage of assessments completed on time because their local authority has been criticised for its record in this, and is itself under pressure. However, Gill knows that by cutting corners, she is placing children at risk, as well as placing herself at risk of being accused of professional incompetence, should a child be harmed as a result of an inadequate assessment. Nevertheless, she continues to do it because she feels it is the only way to get the job done. What might she do differently?

Comments on Exercise 10.4

As we've seen, social workers in this sort of situation may simply do their best to meet the demands of their employer, the local authority, by cutting corners. If a child is harmed as a result of missing information in one of Gill's assessments, though, she can be fairly sure that the local authority will not take responsibility for the poor quality of the assessment and will not publicly admit that she was simply responding to the pressure to complete assessments on time no matter what.

(Cont'd)

On the contrary, she will be held responsible herself, and in some ways rightly so, for she is colluding in a pretence, and has gone along with the dubious priorities that placed being on time above being reliable or useful. We are not suggesting here that she should or could simply flout the demands of the authority, or her manager, and ignore the deadlines, but it would be possible for her to regularly place on record that she is concerned about the quality of her assessments, and that she is only managing to complete them by missing out potentially important sources of information. This would not just be a matter of 'covering her back', though it would certainly help with that. It would also be a case of being true to the 'duty of realism', and refusing to pretend that things are other than they really are. Her manager and her agency might not welcome what she was doing, but in fact she would be being helpful, by providing them with realistic feedback on which they could act, rather than creating an illusion for them that things are different from what they actually are. She cannot control whether they act on this information (any more than the rail engineer, Mr Lewis, referred to above, could control whether Network Rail acted on his warnings), but she can at least provide them with accurate information on which to base their decisions.

CHAPTER SUMMARY

This chapter has discussed the ethical issues that are connected with the allocation of resources within social work and social care. We noted that in many agencies, there is a practitioner–manager split, with managers making resource decisions and practitioners assessing need, but we argued that practitioners too are closely implicated in decisions about resources. We discussed the different philosophical approaches (deontological versus utilitarian) that are typically taken to resource decisions, as well as the different approaches taken in terms of policy.

We looked at the tension between acting as a wholehearted advocate for your client, and working for the fairest and most equitable distribution of resources. We discussed the responsibility to recognise resource limitations when planning a piece of work. Finally, we discussed the importance of speaking out about situations where resources are not sufficient for the job, rather than colluding in a pretence that they are.

 FURTHER READING

We have not identified any recent book specifically focusing on resource decisions in social work and social care (though as we have noted, there are a number of books written from a health perspective). The report below, commissioned by the Commission for Social Care Inspection, and referred to several times in this chapter, is perhaps the nearest thing:

Hudson, B. and Henwood, M. (2008) *Prevention, Personalisation and Prioritisation in Social Care: Squaring the Circle?* London: Commission for Social Care Inspection.

11

DIFFERENCE AND DIVERSITY

- Differences, diversity and discrimination
- Being discriminating and being discriminatory
- Dimensions of difference
- The benefits of difference and diversity

The lamps are different. But the light is the same. (from 'One, One, One' by Jalalu'l-Din Rumi [1207–1273] (Nicholson, 1995: 166)

This thirteenth century Muslim poet provides a reminder to twenty-first century readers that there is something unique and different about every human being – the two authors of this book are a case in point, coming from different ethnic backgrounds, born in different countries, and subscribing to different belief systems – but, at the same time, behind the uniqueness and difference of every human being is a core of likeness. As a student of Andrew's once observed, perhaps a little less poetically than Rumi, 'the paintwork might be different outside but underneath we are all the same'.

That is not always how it seems, though. We are surrounded by difference: different genders, different abilities, different backgrounds, different sexual preferences, different beliefs, different opinions, different tastes and interests, different cultural practices. No two people are quite the same, and this presents us with a lot of challenges. As we discussed in Chapter 9, there is a tendency in human beings to 'other' or 'objectify' groups of people who they see as different to themselves, allowing us to apply different standards to them as if they were not fellow human beings, or at any rate not equivalent to ourselves. We are prone, too, to judge those we have identified as 'other' by different, and often less tolerant, standards to those by which we judge ourselves. (When our side drops a bomb on civilians, it is legitimate warfare, but when the other side do it, they are murderers or terrorists; when I am late for an appointment, it is because I am very busy, but when the client is late it demonstrates lack of commitment.) This is something that has been recognised for a long time, and it happens at the personal as well as the group level. (Anyone who has a long-term partner will surely know that it is often much easier to notice our loved one's annoying habits than it is to recognise our own.) 'Why do you look at the speck of sawdust in your brother's eye,' runs a famous passage written almost two millennia ago in the Christian Gospels, 'and pay no attention to the plank in your own eye?' (Matthew 7: 3).

This chapter will consider some of the implications of the fact that every human society has to deal with difference. It is an appropriate subject with which to end a book on values and ethics because, in the end, the reason we need to think about ethics at all is the simple fact that, as Zygmunt Bauman put it, 'to live is to live *with others*' (1993: 146, original emphasis).

EXERCISE 11.1

THE EXPERIENCE OF BEING DIFFERENT

Consider the following situations:

- You are visiting a city and manage to get completely lost. In the part of the city where you find yourself, you become aware that you are the person on the street who looks the way you do (you are the only white person, or the only black person). You are surrounded by people who look different from you and speak to one another in a language which you don't understand. You need help in finding your way back to where you started from.
- You are invited to a formal occasion – a wedding perhaps, or a funeral. When you get there, you realise that you have not understood what the dress code was for the occasion. You are dressed completely differently from everyone else.
- You find yourself in a social gathering where everyone else present is a member of a different social class from yourself (you are the only working-class person at a party of middle-class people, perhaps, or vice versa).
- You are the only man in a gathering of women – or the only woman in a gathering of men.
- You are the only white person in a gathering of black people, or vice versa.

(Or, if you can think of better examples of situations where you were aware of being *different*, think about those.)

What feelings come up in situations such as these? How do you react? What strategies do you adopt?

Comments on Exercise 11.1

We would suggest that all these situations have, at the very least, the potential to be uncomfortable. We would guess that most readers of this book will have had some experiences of this kind that did not just feel uncomfortable, but were downright frightening. Often what we are afraid of in these sorts of situation is ridicule, humiliation or rejection.

But we would guess too that most people have had at least some experience of being in situations of this kind and fearing for their actual physical safety. Sometimes those fears may have been justified. There really are situations where simply being different places us in physical – even mortal – danger. Sometimes those fears have not been justified but we feel them nevertheless.

As we have already observed, everyone has these experiences – no one can go through life feeling all the time that they are part of the majority – some groups of people are placed in these kinds of situations much more often than others. Of the authors of this book, for instance, Andrew – as a black man living in a country which is more than 90% white – will obviously far more frequently have experiences of this kind than a white man such as Chris. For those who do not have such experiences so often, imagination is called for in appreciating the position of those who do.

As to how we react in these kinds of situation, there seem to be a number of possibilities. Sometimes people try and hide their differences (consider gay people who choose not to disclose the fact that they are gay), or minimise them, or even 'curry favour' with the majority group (consider the way that some men in a predominantly female context – such as a social work office – make self-deprecating remarks about men in an effort to identify themselves as different from other men). Sometimes people react defensively, become prickly and hostile and even exaggerate their differences (consider the way that some working-class people in a middle-class context may feel the need to exaggerate their working-class accent in order to emphasise their difference from those around them).

This exercise demonstrates, we hope, that, whether we like it or not, being different can be difficult. It *matters* to us. In the exercise, we considered the experience of being in a minority and the fact that it feels uncomfortable. Perhaps a second exercise may help to illustrate just *why* it feels uncomfortable. We suspect that this exercise is probably also rather more uncomfortable to do.

THINGS YOU DON'T LIKE ABOUT *THEM*

Being as honest with yourself as you can be, try and think of one thing that you sometimes find yourself disliking or being annoyed or irritated by, about the following:

- people of the opposite gender to yourself;
- old people – or young people if you consider yourself to be old;

EXERCISE 11.2

(Cont'd)

- people with disabilities – or people with different disabilities to yourself;
- people who belong to a different ethnic group to yourself;
- people from a different social class.

Comments on Exercise 11.2

We suspect that most people will not have had much difficulty in thinking of something that they dislike or are annoyed by in each of these categories.

It is not so difficult to imagine, we suggest, how these minor dislikes and irritations can, under certain circumstances, grow into something more sinister.

DIFFERENCES, DIVERSITY AND DISCRIMINATION

It is a fact of human existence that everyone's experience is unique. No one can know exactly what it feels like to be another person. This is at the same time useful ('horses for courses', as the saying goes), fascinating, exasperating, a threat, exciting, lonely, a source of comfort and a source of oppression and cruelty. The difference between the sexes, for instance, is often the basis for love, attraction and fascination, but a huge source too of misunderstandings, assumptions, exasperation and pain. It has also been the basis of all sorts of unfair discrimination and abuse.

To understand the existence of difference is to challenge what we perceive as our own identity. If someone makes different choices to me, perhaps that means my choices are wrong? If someone believes something different to me, are they calling my beliefs untrue? If someone speaks a different language, how can I be sure of what they are saying? The more unknown and different the other person is, the less they fit in with the system of classification by which we order our lives, the greater is the challenge. 'The stranger carries a threat of wrong classification,' Bauman observes, 'but – more horrifying yet – she is a threat to classification as such, to the order of the universe ...' (1993: 150). If that sounds a little 'over the top', pause for a moment and reflect on the cruel and savage things that people have done to other people, throughout history, just for being a little different to themselves. Difference very easily becomes a pretext for oppression, and it can become a reason for discounting people, failing to hear or to notice them, and failing to recognise that their point of view is as valid as our own.

This can happen at an individual level – John fails to listen to Susan's point of view because she is a woman, Lucy doesn't notice Michael because he is disabled, Roger discounts Tommy's opinion because he is only a child, Philip discounts Roland's views and feelings because Roland is black: in all kinds of circumstances, one person may discount the views and feelings of others because of some perceived difference – but it can also happen at the structural level. Groups and categories of human beings can be excluded explicitly (as in apartheid South Africa) or implicitly (as in modern

Britain) from full participation in society. Discrimination at the structural level in turn feeds back into individual acts of discrimination. John might be more inclined to ignore Susan's point of view on political matters if he lived in a society – such as Britain until 1926 – where women were not entitled to vote in elections on the grounds that politics was not for women ...

Dealing with difference will certainly be an issue for you in your professional life as a social worker, for it is a job that will bring you face to face with people who are very different to you in all kinds of ways, and yet require you, if you are to do your job properly, to try and understand their viewpoint at a very personal level: not just 'being aside' them, as Bauman calls it, or 'being with' them, but 'being for' them (1995). For these reasons, any discussion about values and ethics in social work needs to include some reflection on the issues raised by the fact of difference and diversity.

BEING DISCRIMINATING AND BEING DISCRIMINATORY

The word 'discrimination' is a somewhat confusing one. We need to be clear that to discriminate between people is very much part of a social worker's job. Social workers *need* to discriminate between one person and another – taking into account a whole range of factors including class and culture, as well as individual life history – if they are to provide a good service tailored to an individual's needs. Indeed, the purpose of a social work assessment is to help social work agencies to discriminate between one person and another. As Neil Thompson says, 'the literal meaning of discrimination is to identify a difference. As such it is not necessarily a negative term' (Thompson, 2006: 12).

Discrimination, etc.

Discriminate: 1 'recognise a distinction; differentiate ...'; 2 'make an unjust or prejudicial distinction in the treatment of different categories of people, especially on the grounds of race, sex or age'. (*Oxford Dictionary of English*, 2009)

So the word has a neutral meaning ('recognise a distinction') and a negative meaning ('make an unjust or prejudicial distinction'). Discrimination also has a positive meaning of 'having or showing refined taste or good judgement'. (*OED*, 2009)

Discriminatory has the purely negative meaning of 'making or showing an unfair or prejudicial distinction between different categories of people or things'. (*OED*, 2009)

Positive discrimination is a term used to describe acts of discrimination intended to have desirable consequences for a group which has been discriminated against – for instance: reserving certain jobs for people from ethnic minorities who are under-represented in the workforce.

So when we talk about 'anti-discriminatory practice' (another one of those social work buzzwords, of course, as we have observed before), we are not talking about practice that refuses to discriminate between people – that would simply be incompetent! – but about practice that recognises, takes seriously, avoids and tries to challenge *unfair, unjust* and *unwarranted* discrimination. For a nursery school or an old people's home to use age as a criterion of admission is not unwarranted, since nursery schools and old people's homes have specific briefs to meet the needs of certain age groups. For them to use ethnic origin as a criterion *would*, generally speaking, be unwarranted – and in fact would also be illegal in the UK under a series of laws dating back to the 1965 Race Relations Act. (The 2010 Equality Act has recently harmonised a wide range of such legislation with the intention of helping to sever the link between difference and inequality by requiring equal treatment in access to employment and services, regardless of age, disability, gender, sexual orientation, religion or belief, ethnicity and other forms of difference.)

This is not to say, for instance, that it would be discriminatory for (say) a white foster carer to seek special help in caring for the hair of her black foster children, because this would simply be a reflection of her own lack of knowledge and of the fact that different children have different needs. On the other hand, for her to show favouritism and give preferential treatment to white children over black ones (or vice versa), or boys over girls (or vice versa) *would be* unwarranted discrimination.

So, recognising diversity and responding to difference – in face-to-face work and in the planning of services – is good practice. In fact, this is necessary if we are genuinely to show 'respect for others'. However, using difference as a basis for providing a preferential service to some groups is bad practice, contrary to the principle of respect for others, contrary to social justice, and indeed, as we have seen, contrary to the law.

DIMENSIONS OF DIFFERENCE

People differ from one another in literally countless ways, any one of which has the potential to be a basis of discrimination. If you consider hair colour, for example, you will see that there are certain stereotypical assumptions that are made about 'blondes' and 'redheads'. However, we will now look at dimensions of difference where unfair discrimination has a strong structural and historic component, and is therefore something that occurs systematically. In all of these dimensions, discriminatory assumptions are so widespread that we can take it virtually as a certainty that we actually hold some of those assumptions ourselves, whether we want to or not. It may be helpful to start by considering your own position.

YOUR PLACE IN THE DIMENSIONS OF DIFFERENCE

The 'dimensions of difference', which we are now about to discuss (sociologists refer to these as 'social divisions' [Payne, 2006]), are 'ethnicity/race', 'class', 'gender', 'disability' and 'age'. A small part of your own individual identity is measurable along these dimensions. (You must have an age, a gender and an ethnic background. You will have ideas about your class background. You may or may not have a disability.)

You will also have personal circumstances which affect the way you see others who are different from you. You might have a sibling or a child who is disabled, for instance. You might have a close friend who has a different ethnic background to yourself.

You may also feel that there are other 'dimensions' which are very important to your identity but which we have not mentioned here. You may be gay or lesbian. Or you may have suffered from a mental illness and feel that marks you out, in some senses, as different from other people. You may have religious beliefs which are an important part of your sense of yourself.

What we would like you to do is to reflect on where you are located on these various dimensions and consider how you relate to others who are differently located. (If you are black, how do you relate to people who are white, for instance? If you are not disabled, how do you relate to people who are?)

Along which of these dimensions do you think you find it most difficult to empathise with people who are different from you? For example, perhaps you are a woman and find it particularly hard to recognise and/or care about specific issues that are experienced by men in this society. If so, you are identifying the dimension of gender as particularly difficult for you.

Comments on Exercise 11.3

Social workers do not do service users justice if they assume that their own particular perspective, based on their own limited life experience, is somehow the right one. For instance, a white person may have difficulty in really understanding what it means to be a black person on the receiving end of racism, and therefore may be inclined to dismiss it as not a serious problem, but this would be a failure to respect the experiences of others. It is important to notice and make allowances for our own 'blind spots'.

ETHNICITY/RACE

Racism

Many definitions of racism could be offered, not all of which completely agree with each other.

(Cont'd)

> Our suggestion is:
>
> Ideology based on the proposition that a certain ethnic group can be superior or inferior in worth to others.
>
> Historically, racism was based on alleged biological differences between the races, making some races allegedly inherently inferior to others, but, as Simon Clark points out, there has been a subtle shift in racist ideology. The 'New Racism' relies less on alleged biological differences and concentrates instead on 'cultural differences in which the Other becomes demonised' (2003: 8). Indeed, the New Racist may actually claim not to be a racist, but merely to be concerned to protect his or her culture.

There are visible differences between human beings whose ancestors originated in different parts of the world, and there are also differences in beliefs, language, customs and norms of day-to-day behaviour. In any situation where people from different ethnic backgrounds live alongside one another, there is the potential for prejudice, conflict and for the oppression of one group by another. Anti-Semitism and prejudice against gypsies are examples of prejudice which are still widespread, and both of which, only half a century ago, were used by the Nazis as a pretext for mass murder.

In the huge movements of peoples that took place during the colonial and postcolonial eras, literally hundreds of millions of people were transplanted across the globe as a result of colonial conquest, slavery and mass migration. A consequence of this is that most Western countries are multi-cultural to a greater extent than ever before. People in Western countries have had to become accustomed to living alongside people who look different to themselves and have different traditions and beliefs. As we have seen, difference is, for various reasons, often experienced as a threat, which means that creating a harmonious multi-cultural and multi-racial society presents us with many challenges.

Difference is always difficult – even within a marriage, after all, or between the members of a family, differences present us with challenges – but in the UK context, the prejudices that exist among the white population about black and Asian people have a number of specific features. Black and Asian people are readily recognisable as different from the majority population (unlike, say, people of Polish descent), and black and Asian people, even after living in the UK for generations, continue to be seen by some as incomers, in a way that generally does not happen with second- and third-generation white immigrants (which is not to say that white minority groups, such as travellers, or people of Irish or Polish origin, do not also face discrimination). In particular, black and Asian people have to deal not only with the ignorant and unfair prejudices which tend to be faced by any identifiably different group, but with the lingering remnants of the ideology of racism which, as we discussed in Chapter 9, provided the rationale for slavery and colonial rule in Africa and Asia.

Although racism is no longer an officially sanctioned ideology (and, in the UK and other countries, racial discrimination is against the law), it has had a huge and pervasive influence on our culture. This means that we as individuals – black and white – will all hold assumptions which we are not necessarily ourselves aware of, which are likely to affect our practice and decision making about black and Asian service users in particular. These kinds of assumptions also permeate the institutions and structures of our society, in the form of institutional racism.

Institutional racism

'The collective failure of an organisation to provide an appropriate and professional ser-vice to people because of their colour, culture or ethnic origin. It can be seen or detected in processes, attitudes and behaviour which amount to discrimination through unwit-ting prejudice, ignorance, thoughtlessness and racist stereotyping which disadvantage minority ethnic people'. (*The Stephen Lawrence Enquiry*, Macpherson [1999: 28]) (At the time of writing, two of Stephen Lawrence's killers have finally been convicted of murder, 18 years after his death.)

Institutional racism is about customary attitudes, mindsets and ways of behaving that are perpetuated by a 'it's just the way we do things around here' mentality – that allows individual prejudice to go uncensored and to take root in the fabric of an organisation.

Because of the structural character of racism, it is not sufficient simply for the social worker to be 'colour-blind' when dealing with service users, and refuse to take account of people's skin colour or ethnicity at all, since that would entail also being 'blind' to much of the service user's experience. In particular, it would entail ignor-ing the possibility that racism was a significant part of that experience. The follow-ing exercise may help to illustrate this:

DEALING WITH RACIST BULLYING

You are a residential social worker in an assessment unit for adolescents. Most of your resi-dents are white, while some are black. The black residents are coming in for some bullying from some of the white ones, and this includes racial abuse.

What would be a 'colour-blind' way of dealing with this?

What would be a way of dealing with this that took into account that the recipients of the bullying were 'members of an oppressed group'?

EXERCISE 11.4

Comments on Exercise 11.4

You may well have more ideas than we have about how to deal with such behaviour in a residential establishment. However, we would suggest that either approach would involve trying to deal with the bullying, perhaps by making arrangements to support and protect the victims and by challenging the bullies, perhaps by imposing restrictions or sanctions on them, or perhaps by trying to work with the residents as a group to find their own solutions.

However, a 'colour-blind' approach would involve dealing with the bullying as bullying, and name calling as name calling, without paying attention to its racist content or to the fact that its victims are exclusively black and its perpetrators exclusively white.

The alternative anti-racist approach, would recognise that racism was as much of an issue here as bullying and therefore needed tackling as a distinct and separate issue. By putting racist name calling on a par with other kinds of name calling, the colour-blind approach is ignoring the fact that racist abuse is not just a personal thing between two groups of boys but part of a pervasive pattern in which black people are given negative messages about themselves. So, the anti-racist approach would need to give a strong message that racist put-downs, not just bullying, were unacceptable in this environment.

As for putting it to the whole resident's group as a problem to solve, this would clearly be inappropriate if the resident group, in which white children are in the majority, was polarised further into 'them and us', white and black. The black residents would then find themselves in a position of being outnumbered and might fear that other non-bullying white residents might side with the bullies rather than with them, or at least be inclined to minimise the bullies' activities. There is also a danger that those not involved may consider they too are being blamed as the perpetrators and join the others in the bullying behaviour.

CLASS

Curiously, class is very often forgotten in discussions about difference and anti-discriminatory practice. Neil Thompson's *Anti-discriminatory Practice* (2006), for instance, includes chapters on gender, ethnicity, age and disability, but, although class is mentioned, it does not get a chapter on its own. This seems odd, because a considerable number of social work service users are white, male, young and able-bodied, but are still disadvantaged because of poverty and social disadvantage. Even for service users who are women, black, elderly or disabled, social class makes a huge amount of difference to the opportunities available to them, and the discrimination they will face.

For statistical purposes, 'class' tends to be defined by income or by occupation, but in our encounters with other people, we in Britain evaluate 'class' or 'status' in rather more complex ways. The words 'posh' or 'common', for instance, as used in everyday speech to locate people along the dimension of class, refer to more than just money and jobs. (Students often raise the case of the billionaire businessman, Alan Sugar: immensely wealthy, and now a member of the House of Lords, but not really describable as 'posh'.) Britain is said to be a particularly class-conscious society as compared to North America or continental Europe, but certainly in British society the social class of a person, like their ethnic origin, is something that we deduce from a whole range of cues, including dress, body language, consumer choices – such as choice of newspaper, house décor or car – and accent (for more on this, see Scott, 2006). Working-class people in England, for instance, tend to speak with regional accents which not only identify their class but also roughly which part of the country they come from. Middle-class people – and certainly those who come from established middle-class families – characteristically speak a form of English which linguists know as RP (Received Pronunciation). Even within RP there are regional variations but they are not very pronounced, with the result that it is often hard to place the geographical origin of an RP speaker. But, while we cannot necessarily place an RP speaker geographically, we do in British society tend to assume that an RP speaker is well-educated and belongs to the middle class. The accent is commonly referred to not only as 'posh' but as 'being well-spoken', with the implication, of course, that other accents are 'badly spoken'.

The RP accent is associated with people in powerful, prominent positions: doctors, teachers, judges, politicians, television announcers, clergymen, senior businessmen. It is so rarely associated with people doing low-paid or menial tasks that if we heard, say, a street cleaner talking in that way, we would instantly notice it, just as we would instantly notice a prominent judge speaking in a broad regional accent. In other words, RP is associated with power and privilege.

We suggest that if you speak with an RP accent and work in a field such as children and family social work, whose service users tend to come predominantly from poor working-class backgrounds, then the way you speak will be noted as an indicator of difference and a reminder of your powerful position. Even if you *don't* speak with an RP accent, other cues such as your dress and even just the fact that you are a social worker will be read in this way.

You too (we suggest) will inevitably be aware of class differences, just as you will be aware of difference when working with people from a different ethnic background to yourself. There are real dangers of stereotyping people on the basis of the fact that they are a different class to yourself, or of giving preferential treatment to those you recognise as having a similar background because you find it easier to identify with their situation. We have also many times heard social workers and social work students comment that they are more self-conscious and careful about their practice when dealing with middle-class service users because they are aware that middle-class people tend to be more confident about asserting their rights. This gives some indication of how much social workers normally feel protected by the fact of their powerful position and their social status when they are dealing with poor and working-class families.

It's also important to bear in mind that different classes, like different ethnic groups, have their own cultures and different priorities. Shor (2000), for instance, shows how families from different neighbourhoods have different views about what constitutes child maltreatment.

Stereotypes

'[a] widely held but fixed and oversimplified image or idea of a particular type of person or thing'. (*Oxford Dictionary of English*, 2009)

A stereotype is a form of generalisation. Generalisations are normal and necessary to learning. For example, a child who touches something hot avoids burning herself by generalising this experience to other similar experiences.

However, generalisations about different groups of human beings, even if they have some basis in fact (which is often not the case), are dangerous because they have the effect of shutting us off from contrary experience. If we are convinced that all young men in hoodies are criminals, for instance, we will tend not to notice or will discount evidence to the contrary.

The effect of this can be deeply oppressive for the person on the receiving end, who is denied the option of being accepted for who they actually are.

Making guesses, and forming hypotheses about other people, is something that we inevitably do. It is when these guesses and hypotheses acquire a sense of permanency and resistance to change that they become stereotypes: the basis upon which labels are attached and from which generalisations are made and sustained.

GENDER

Each one of the 'dimensions of difference' which we are discussing has its own distinctive characteristics, meaning that it cannot be regarded as exactly comparable to the others. What is different about gender, as compared to ethnicity and class, is that men and women do not live in separate communities and separate dwellings. Most households include both men and women. Most of us have men and women among the people we most care about. All of us have both a mother and a father. If we are parents, whether a father or a mother, we may have sons or daughters or both, and usually love all of them. (We don't dispute that many people have friends and loved ones from different class and ethnic backgrounds: we just make the point that many people don't.)

In spite of the close proximity between men and women and the many close ties that cross the gender line, this dimension of difference is the source of unwarranted discrimination and real oppression.

Sex and gender

Sex refers to the biological difference between male and female.

Gender refers to the different roles and characteristics assigned in a social context to the biological sexes. Many of these characteristics (perhaps most) are social in origin rather than biological, the products of 'nature' rather than 'nurture'.

Both men and women suffer as a result of the restricted roles and expectations to which socially constructed ideas about gender consign them. However, there is no doubt that the most obvious victims of sexism are women. Women are paid less than men, are under-represented at, or absent from, the senior levels of most organisations (including social services departments), and they are over-represented in low-paid, low status work such as, in the social care context, care assistance. They also do more housework than men (Abbott, 2006: 83). They face expectations that they are responsible for the care of children and of other relatives such as frail elderly parents, or adults with disabilities, and face much more pressure than men do to make this their priority (consider the judgement that society makes of a woman who walks out on her children, as compared to that made about a man who does so). They are the main victims of rape and sexual assault, and may face humiliation and disbelief in a male-dominated court system if they try and bring their attackers to justice. They are also the main victims of domestic violence. It is possible to think of contexts in which men may feel disadvantaged or excluded, but these tend to be at the cultural and individual level, while discrimination against women exists at the institutional or structural level.

Sexism

'prejudice, stereotyping, or discrimination, typically against women, on the basis of sex'. (*Oxford Dictionary of English*, 2009)

In practice, the word refers to the inequitable and unjust treatment of women by men, though in principle it could refer to unjust treatment of men by women.

Social work is in an interesting position in relation to sexism because it operates in the 'caring' sphere, which has traditionally been assigned to women. In Britain, the majority of social workers, like nurses, are women – according to Perry and Cree (2003), 86% of applications for social work courses in 2000 were from women, and our impression is that this situation is probably broadly unchanged today – though this ratio does not continue into senior management (there were, for instance, four men out of seven board members of the Association of Directors of Children's Services listed on the ADCS website as of February 2012 [ADCS, undated]). And, although social workers deal with men and women, boys and girls, as service users, the *carers of others* that they deal with are mainly women. As representatives of a state welfare system which does not provide care on demand to any user group, but rations it tightly on the basis of need, social workers will often find themselves in the position of trying to encourage women carers to 'hang in there' in the absence of a viable alternative.

This can put social workers on the horns of a dilemma in which, in order to protect the interests of their service user as best they can, they may have to effectively exploit women by prevailing on their goodwill or their conscience. The example in the following exercise illustrates this:

PRESSURE ON SUE TO CARE

Aged 46, the youngest of four, and the only girl, in a suburban white British family, Sue grew up with parents who pushed their sons to achieve, and seemed to value their daughter's achievements very little. Sue didn't leave home until the age of 24 when she married an older man and became a housewife and mother. Her children have both now grown up and left home and she has recently started a job as a learning support assistant in a local school, her first paid work since before she married, which she very much enjoys.

However, her mother has now suddenly died and her father, Mr Roberts, suffers from advanced Parkinson's disease. He is in need of daily personal care. Sue's three brothers expect Sue to give up her part-time job to care for him, pointing out that all three of them are the main breadwinners for their families, while Sue's income is small and she is supported finan-cially by her husband. The only alternative is for Mr Roberts to go into a residential home and it is agreed between Sue and her brothers that this would literally kill him, as he is a fiercely independent man who would hate institutional care.

Sue agrees with her brothers about her duty, but the prospect fills her with such dread that she can't sleep at nights and has asked her GP for sleeping pills.

You are the care co-ordinator for Mr Roberts. You know that your agency will not be able to fund sufficient domiciliary care to keep Mr Roberts at home without additional input from Sue. His care needs are such that a complete domiciliary care package would actually be more costly than residential care, so the latter is the only alternative. What would you do?

Comments on Exercise 11.5

In a real-life situation of this kind, you might well feel that you were left with no option but to leave the burden of decision on the shoulders of Sue, in essence giving her the message:

> 'Either let your father go into residential care and be blamed by your brothers and yourself for his subsequent deterioration, or once again give up the possi-bility of a career of your own to provide care for your family!'

As care co-ordinator for Mr Roberts, your primary responsibility is to him as a service user, but you do also have legal duties to assess Sue's needs as a carer under the 1995 Carers (Recognition and Services) Act. Unfortunately, this does not necessarily mean your agency is going to be able to meet those needs.

Perhaps, though, there is a way of challenging the assumptions of Sue's brothers that this is all down to her? Perhaps you could call a family conference, enlisting the GP's help to underline concerns about Sue's health, and pushing for a solution in which all family mem-bers contribute time and/or money to put with whatever help your agency is able to give?

DISABILITY

> ### Disablism
>
> '... systematic discrimination and prejudice against people with disabilities which produce a milieu of oppression and degradation'. (Thompson, 2006: 122)

We live in what could be described as a disabling society, in that people who have physical, sensory or learning impairments of one kind or another are frequently denied access to many of the things other people casually take for granted. It is this lack of access, rather than just the impairment itself, that results in disability. The ways in which access is restricted vary from physical obstacles, such as stairs and doorways that cannot be used by people in wheelchairs, to discrimination in selection processes such as job interviews, to a more subtle and pervasive message that comes from public attitudes encountered on the streets and in the media.

Social workers supporting people with learning, physical and sensory disabilities will be very aware of the difficulties that disabled people typically face to achieve many things in life that non-disabled people would regard as normal. Historically, these difficulties would have been seen as sad consequences of the individual's impairments, and the social worker could be seen as reflecting society's benevolent wish to 'help' these 'unfortunate' people.

In recent times, some disabled people have challenged this way of seeing things and effectively turned it on its head, pointing out that their lack of access to work, public buildings, public transport, and so on is not an inevitable consequence of, say, being blind or having non-functioning legs, but is the result of the rest of society failing to make access possible. On this argument, disability is in fact a social construction, a particular way in which society responds to people with impairments, and, far from expressing society's benevolence, the services that are made available to disabled people represent crumbs thrown down from a table to which disabled people should rightfully have full access. In this new analysis, 'disability is defined as a form of social exclusion and oppression. Political campaigns called for a "rights not charity" approach' (Mercer, 2002: 117). The logic of this approach suggests the need for a concept analogous to 'sexism' or 'racism' to describe the ideological system which justifies the exclusion of disabled people from society: hence 'disablism'.

In fact, 'disablism' has been responsible for rather more active forms of oppression than just failing to provide access. Disabled people in the UK are regularly the target of bullying and indeed are sometimes even murdered (see Shakespeare, 2010), because of their disability. Here, for instance, are some accounts given by parents of disabled children and young people of the kinds of abuse to which their children have been subjected:

> The youth worker called me into her office. She looked dreadful, shocked. Eventually she told me that there had been an incident in the toilet. A group of girls had been teasing Isobel and they tried to get her to lick the toilet seat ...

> She's had her moments [says another parent], she got bullied by a girl on the school bus, they pinned her down and were putting tampons in her mouth …
> (both examples taken from Goodley and Runswick-Cole, 2011: 606)

Disabled people, like Jews and gypsies, were sent to Nazi death camps. Even in the UK, in 1909, Winston Churchill suggested the compulsory sterilisation of 'mental defectives' (see Gilbert, 2009). In fairness to him, he thought (possibly correctly) this might be more humane than another alternative, which was to effectively incarcerate large numbers of men and women in institutions where the sexes were rigidly segregated to prevent them from reproducing, including many who we would now regard as having extremely mild learning difficulties, or as simply not being of very high intelligence. This second alternative was actually implemented and many people institutionalised in this way remained so into the 1980s.

In the face of a history of humiliating and infantilising treatment of disabled people, and continued exclusion of disabled people from full participation in society, the social worker seeking to counter 'disablism' has to try to radically rethink his traditional role from paternalistic helper to enabler, advocate or ally (see, for instance, Brandon et al., 1995).

AGE

Age is a common basis for unwarranted discrimination and has accordingly been given its own 'ism'.

Ageism

'Prejudice or discrimination on the grounds of a person's age'. (*Oxford Dictionary of English*, 2009)

The word is most usually used to refer to the treatment of older people, but 'children and young people can also be the victims of ageist attitudes and practices'. (Thompson, 2005: 5)

We have visited residential homes for the elderly which seemed more like warehouses for the storage of entities who would otherwise be an inconvenience. This is not by any means true of all such homes, of course, but when it happens it surely constitutes a breakdown of 'respect for persons', with people no longer really being valued as 'ends' in their own right, except in so far as society recognises an obligation to keep them physically alive. The gradual shift from autonomous human being to an entity whose fate is to be decided by others to suit their own convenience, is a shift which many old people experience at earlier stages than actual admission to residential care. And discrimination against old people, it can be argued, occurs at a structural as well as at an individual level. (The odd thing about ageism, of course, is that when we 'other' the elderly, we are othering, not strangers, but our own future selves. Some would argue that ageism against the elderly results from 'deep-rooted irrational fears of our own ageing, and our apprehension at the prospect of physical and mental decay' [Macnicol, 2006: 9].) One challenge for social workers working with older people is to carry out their function of rationing and managing limited care resources while still holding onto the idea that old people are people, entitled to their own views and opinions, and not just logistical problems to be solved. (See the case of Ruby, for example, who we discussed in Exercise 4.3 on page 57.)

Social workers in work with children likewise have to work hard not to be deflected by the needs of other, often more vocal, family members or indeed by the demands of other professionals and their own agency, from retaining a focus on the needs and perspective of the child. They also have to be careful to remember, as Dame Elizabeth Butler-Sloss commented in the Cleveland report, 'The child is a person and not an object of concern' (1987: 245).

THE BENEFITS OF DIFFERENCE AND DIVERSITY

We have been discussing the ways in which people from various groups may be discriminated against and oppressed by other groups, but it would be a rather negative and one-sided view of difference and diversity that dwelt only on the problems that difference can cause for those who are seen as 'different'. As we said at the beginning of the chapter, difference is a challenge for all of us, but we should not lose sight of the fact that it is also a source of comfort and delight. Within every family and every group of friends, people are different from one another in all kinds of ways, and this is something that gives us pleasure and is often helpful to us, even if it is sometimes also the source of tensions and misunderstanding.

Presented with a salad, most of us would feel disappointed if it contained nothing but identical lettuce leaves. In the same way, most of us would find life rather sad and dull if we never met people who differed from us in any way. So working with difference and diversity is not just a matter of challenging unfair discrimination, important though that is. It is also a matter of positively celebrating diversity.

Genuine respect for persons entails recognising and accepting difference, both at an individual level and at the level of structures, policies and institutions, and it means recognising that people in different circumstances and with different backgrounds have different needs. It also means recognising that people in different circumstances have different things to *contribute*, and that society as a whole benefits from diversity. It is a cliché but nevertheless true that 'it takes all sorts to make a world'.

CHAPTER SUMMARY

This chapter has looked at the implications for social work practice raised by the existence of difference and diversity in society. We began by noting that dealing with difference is one of the challenges of human life, and is particularly a challenge for social workers, who need to work with people who may be very different from themselves, on issues that may be intimate and personal.

We have noted that discriminating between one person and another is, of itself, not a bad thing, and in fact is necessary and important, but we made a distinction between being discriminating and being *discriminatory*, the latter referring to unfair and unwarranted discrimination. We have discussed ethnicity, class, gender, disability and age as bases for unfair discrimination, though we could have looked at many other social divisions or 'dimensions of difference', as we called them (religion, nationality, sexual orientation, mental health ... the list is endless).

However, we concluded this chapter (and this whole book) by pointing out that it would be rather negative to associate difference and diversity simply with problems of discrimination and oppression. It is important as well to recognise that difference and diversity are necessary and valuable, even 'the spice of life'. They may be challenges, but they are not really problems at all.

 FURTHER READING

The following text provides a helpful introduction to the subject of social divisions:

Payne, G. (2006) *Social Divisions*, 2nd edn. Basingstoke: Palgrave.

Neil Thompson's book, now in its fourth edition, remains a standard text on anti-discriminatory practice:

Thompson, N. (2006) *Anti-discriminatory Practice*, 4th edn. Basingstoke: Palgrave.

AFTERWORD

In the Introduction to this book, we said that there was no simple rule or formula that can be applied to tell us the right thing to do, and no alternative to constantly thinking and rethinking the principles and assumptions which form the basis of our actions. Being a genuinely good social worker, we believe, is not about proudly holding up a flag marked 'social work values' as a sign of your essential goodness, but rather about constantly asking yourself 'What ought I to do here? What are the important issues? What action would I be justified in taking here and why?'

We would like to think that this book (in conjunction, of course, with everything else you have read and listened to and discussed as part of your training) has provided you with a little foretaste of what this process of thinking and rethinking might entail, and at least some preparation for your future career. It is a future in which you will not be dealing with imaginary case examples printed in books, which sit there unchanged on the page no matter what you decide, but with real live human beings, whose lives really will be changed, for better or for worse, and sometimes completely transformed, by the thinking you do and the choices you make.

REFERENCES

Abbott, P. (2006) 'Gender', in G. Payne (ed.) *Social Divisions*. Basingstoke: Palgrave, pp. 65–101.

ADCS (Associated of Directors of Children's Services) (undated) Available at: www.adcs.org.uk (accessed February 2012).

Ahmad, B. (1990) Black *Perspectives in Social Work*. Birmingham: Venture Press.

Amphlett, S. (2000) 'System abuse: social violence and families', in H. Payne and B. Littlechild (eds) *Ethical Practice and the Abuse of Power in Social Responsibility*. London: Jessica Kingsley, pp. 175–209.

Annas, J. (2011) *Intelligent Virtue*. Oxford: Oxford University Press.

Bailey, R. and Brake, M. (eds) (1975) *Radical Social Work*. London: Edward Arnold.

Banks, S. (2006) *Ethics and Values in Social Work*, 3rd edn. Basingstoke: Palgrave.

Banks, S. (2009) 'From professional ethics to ethics in professional life: implications for learning, teaching and study', *Ethics and Social Welfare*, 3(1): 55–63.

Banks, S. and Gallagher, A. (2009) *Ethics in Professional Life*. Basingstoke: Palgrave.

Banks, S. and Nøhr, K. (eds) (2011) *Practising Social Work Ethics Around the World: Cases and Commentaries*. London: Routledge.

Banks, S. and Williams, R. (2005) 'Accounting for ethical difficulties in social welfare work: issues, problems and dilemmas', *British Journal of Social Work*, 35(7): 1005–22.

Barn, R. (1993) *Black Children in the Public Care System*. London: Batsford.

Barnado's (2011) *What We Believe*. Available at: www.barnardos.org.uk/who_we_are/what_we_believe.htm (accessed February 2011).

Barnado's (undated) *Our Basis and Values*. Available at: www.barnardos.org.uk/work_with_us/jobs/basis_and_values.htm (accessed July 2011).

Bauman, Z. (1993) *Postmodern Ethics*. Oxford: Blackwell.

Bauman, Z. (1995) *Life in Fragments: Essays in Post-modern Morality*. Oxford: Blackwell.

BBC News (2007) 'Sally Clark dies at family home'. Available at: http://news.bbc.co.uk/1/hi/uk/6460595.stm (accessed October 2011).

BBC News (2008) 'UK apology over rendition flights'. Available at: http://news.bbc.co.uk/1/hi/uk_politics/7256587.stm (accessed October 2011).

BBC News (2011a) 'Timeline of Baby P case'. Available at: www.bbc.co.uk/news/uk-11626806 (accessed October 2011).

BBC News (2011b) 'Grayrigg train crash: faulty points caused woman's death'. Available at: www.bbc.co.uk/news/uk-england-cumbria-15593840 (accessed February 2012).

Beck, U. (1999) *World Risk Society*. Cambridge: Polity.

Beckett, C. (2002) 'The witch-hunt metaphor – and residential workers accused of abuse', *British Journal of Social Work*, 32(5): 621–8.

Beckett, C. (2003) 'The language of siege: military metaphors in the spoken language of social work', *British Journal of Social Work*, 33(5): 625–39.

Beckett, C. (2006) 'Rhetoric and reality', in C. Beckett (ed.) *Essential Theory for Social Work Practice*. London: Sage, pp. 171–84.

Beckett, C. (2007) 'The reality principle: realism as an ethical obligation', *Ethics and Social Welfare*, 1(3): 269–81.

Beckett, C. (2009) 'Realism as an ethical obligation: engaging with practice realities, not just "virtuous words"', *Ethics and Social Welfare*, 3(1): 64–8.

Beckett, C. (2010) *Assessment and Intervention in Social Work: Preparing for Practice.* London: Sage.

Bergeron, L.R. (2008) 'Self-determination and elder abuse: do we know enough?', *Journal of Gerontological Social Work*, 46(3–4): 81–102.

Berlin, I. (1997 [1958]) 'Two concepts of liberty', in *The Proper Study of Mankind.* London: Chatto and Windus, pp. 191–242.

Bhaskar, R. (1989) *Reclaiming Reality.* London: Verso.

Biehal, N., Ellison, S., Baker, C. and Sinclair, I. (2010) *Belonging and Permanence: Outcomes in Long-term Foster Care and Adoption.* London: BAAF.

Biestek, F. (1963) *The Casework Relationship.* St Leonard's: Allen and Unwin.

Birchall, E. and Hallett, C. (1995) *Working Together in Child Protection.* London: HMSO.

Brandon, D. (1990) *Zen in the Art of Helping.* Harmondsworth: Arkana.

Brandon, D. (2000) *Tao of Survival: Spirituality in Social Care and Helping.* Birmingham: Venture.

Brandon, D., Brandon, A. and Brandon, T. (1995) *Advocacy: Power to People with Disabilities.* Birmingham: Venture.

British Association of Social Workers (BASW) (2012) *The Code of Ethics for Social Work.* Birmingham: BASW. Available at: www.basw.co.uk/about/code-of-ethics/ (accessed January 2012).

Broadhurst, K., Wastell, D., White, S., Hall, C., Peckover, S., Thompson, K., Pithouse, A. and Davey, D. (2010) 'Performing "initial assessment": identifying the latent conditions for error at the front-door of local authority children's services', *British Journal of Social Work*, 40(2): 352–70.

Butler, I. and Drakeford, M. (2001) 'Which Blair Project?: communitarianism, social authoritarianism and social work', *Journal of Social Work*, 1(1): 7–19.

Butler-Sloss, Dame E. (1987) *Report of the Inquiry into Child Abuse in Cleveland.* London: HMSO.

Campbell, J. and Davidson, G. (2009) 'Coercion in the community: a situated approach to the examination of ethical challenges for mental health social workers', *Ethics and Social Welfare*, 3(3): 249–63.

Carr, S. (2007) 'Participation, power, conflict and change: theorizing dynamics of service user participation in the social care system of England and Wales', *Critical Social Policy*, 27(2): 266–76.

Chandrasekhar, I., Wardrop, M. and Trotman, A. (2011) 'Phone hacking: timeline of the scandal', *Daily Telegraph*, 10 November. Available at: www.telegraph.co.uk/news/uknews/phone-hacking/8634176/Phone-hacking-timeline-of-a-scandal.html (accessed January 2012).

Children's Legal Centre (2006) *[Summary of] Age Assessment: Joint Working Protocol between IND [Immigration and Nationality Directorate of the Home Office] and ADSS [Association of Directors of Social Services].* Available at: www.childrenslegalcentre.com/OneStopCMS/Core/CrawlerResourceServer.aspx?resource=634EF23E-33E6-48F3-8496-34BC0EF804ED&mode=link&guid=fc8af87a1ce544dea1dd05eb961e2882 (accessed May 2011).

Clark, C. (2000) *Social Work Ethics: Politics, Principles and Practice.* Basingstoke: Palgrave.

Clark, C. (2007) 'Professional responsibility, misconduct and practical reason', *Ethics and Social Welfare*, 1(1): 56–75.

Clark, S. (2003) *Social Theory, Psychoanalysis and Racism*. London: Palgrave Macmillan.

Clifford, D. and Burke, B. (2009) *Anti-oppressive Ethics and Values in Social Work*. Basingstoke: Palgrave.

Cobb, R. and Ross, M. (1997) 'Denying agenda access: strategic considerations', in R. Cobb and M. Ross (eds) *Cultural Strategies of Agenda Denial*. Lawrence, KS: University Press of Kansas, pp. 25–45.

Cohen, S. (2005) *Deportation is Freedom! The Orwellian World of Immigration Controls*. London: Jessica Kingsley.

Cookson, R., McCabe, C. and Tsuchiya, A. (2008) 'Public healthcare resource allocation and the Rule of Rescue', *Journal of Medical Ethics*, 34(7): 540–4.

Craig, G., Gaus, A., Wilkinson, M., Skrivankova, K. and McQuade, A. (2007) *Contemporary Slavery in the UK*. London: Joseph Rowntree Foundation. Available at: ww.jrf.org.uk/sites/files/jrf/2016-contemporary-slavery-uk.pdf (accessed January 2012).

Crawley, H. (2007) *When is a Child not a Child? Asylum, Age Disputes and the Process of Age Assessments*. London: Immigration Law Practitioners Association. Available at: www.ilpa.org.uk/ (accessed April 2010).

Cree, V. (1995) *From Public Streets to Private Lives*. Aldershot: Avebury.

Currie, E. (2010) 'Plain left realism: an appreciation, and some thoughts for the future', *Crime, Law and Social Change*, 54(2): 111–24.

Daily Mail (2005) 'Scandal of the stolen children', *Daily Mail* online. Available at www.dailymail.co.uk/news/article-348650/Scandal-stolen-children.html (accessed August 2011).

Dalrymple, J. and Burke, B. (2006) *Anti-oppressive Practice: Social Care and the Law*, 2nd edn. Maidenhead: McGraw Hill.

Daniels, N. and Sabin, J. (2008) *Setting Limits Fairly: Learning to Share Resources for Health*. Oxford: Oxford University Press.

Davies, H. (2009) 'Ethics and practice in child protection', *Ethics and Social Welfare*, 3(3): 322–8.

Deigh, J. (2010) *An Introduction to Ethics*. Cambridge: Cambridge University Press.

Department for Education (DfE) (2008) *Every Child Matters Outcomes Framework*. Available at: www.education.gov.uk/publications/standard/publicationDetail/Page1/DCSF-00331-2008 (accessed January 2012).

Department of Health (DoH) (2000) *Framework for the Assessment of Children in Need and their Families*. London: TSO.

Department of Health (DoH) (2007) *Putting People First*. London: TSO. Available at: www.dh.gov.uk/en/Publicationsandstatistics/Publications/PublicationsPolicyAndGuidance/DH_081118 (accessed January 2012).

Department of Health (DoH) (2010) *Prioritising Need in the Context of Putting People First: A Whole System Approach to Eligibility in Health and Social Care*. London: TSO.

Dineen, T. (1999) *Manufacturing Victims*. London: Constable.

Dixon, D. (2009) 'When law and ethics collide: social control in child protective services', *Ethics and Social Welfare*, 3(3): 264–83.

Dominelli, L. (2002) *Anti-oppressive Social Work Theory and Practice*. Basingstoke: Palgrave.

Dominelli, L. and McLeod, E. (1989) *Feminist Social Work*. Basingstoke: Macmillan.

Dubois, B. and Miley, K. (2008) *Social Work: An Empowering Profession*, 6th edn. London: Pearson.

Eagleton, T. and Beaumont, M. (2009) *The Task of the Critic: Terry Eagleton in Dialogue*. London: Verso.

Fanon, F. (1967) *Black Skin, White Masks*. New York: Grove Press.

Ferguson, I. (2007) 'Increasing user choice or privatizing risk? The antinomies of personalization', *British Journal of Social Work*, 37(3): 387–403.

Ferguson, I. and Woodward, R. (2009) *Radical Social Work in Practice: Making a Difference*. Bristol: Policy Press.

Foucault, M. (1980) 'Truth and power', in M. Foucault, *Power/Knowledge* (edited by Gordon, C.). Hemel Hempstead: Harvester Wheatsheaf.

Frank, T. (2012) *Pity the Billionaire: The Hard Times Swindle and the Unlikely Comeback of the Right*. London: Harvill Secker.

Fratter, J., Rowe, J., Sapsford, D. and Thoburn, J. (1991) *Permanent Family Placement: A Decade of Experience*. London: BAAF.

Freire, P. (1993) *Pedagogy of the Oppressed*. Harmondsworth: Penguin.

Freud, S. (1923) 'The ego and the id', in J. Strachey (ed.) *Collected Works*, standard edn, Vol. 19. London: Hogarth Press [1961], pp. 3–66.

Furness, S. and Gilligan, P. (2010) *Religion, Belief and Social Work*. Bristol: Policy Press.

General Social Care Council (GSCC) (2010) *Code of Practice for Social Care Workers*. Available at: www.gscc.org.uk/codes/ (accessed October 2011).

Gilbert, M. (2009) *Churchill and Eugenics*. Available at: www.winstonchurchill.org/support/the-churchill-centre/publications/finest-hour-online/594-churchill-and-eugenics (accessed February 2012).

Gilligan, C. (1993) *In a Different Voice*. Cambridge, MA: Harvard University Press.

Gilligan, P. and Furness, S. (2006) 'The role of religion and spirituality in social work practice: views and experiences of social workers and students', *British Journal of Social Work*, 36(4): 617–37.

Girling, J. (1993) 'Who gets what – and why? Ethical frameworks for managers', in I. Allen (ed.) *Rationing of Health and Social Care*. London: Policy Services Institute, pp. 40–7.

Goodley, D. and Runswick-Cole, K. (2011) 'The violence of disablism', *Sociology of Health and Illness*, 33(4): 602–17.

Green, J. (2009) 'The deformation of professional formation: managerial targets and the undermining of professional judgement', *Ethics and Social Welfare*, 3(2): 115–30.

Guardian, The (2011) 'Extraordinary rendition: a backstory', 31 August. Available at: www.guardian.co.uk/world/2011/aug/31/extraordinary-rendition-backstory (accessed October 2011).

Hammersley, M. (1992) *What's Wrong with Ethnography?* London: Routledge.

Hardin, R. (1990) 'The artificial duties of contemporary professionals: the Social Services Review lecture', *Social Service Review*, 64(4): 528–41.

Harne, L. and Radford, J. (2008) *Tackling Domestic Violence: Theories, Policy and Practice*. Maidenhead: Open University Press.

Healy, K. (2008) 'Critical commentary on social work as art revisited', *International Journal of Social Welfare*, 17(2): 194–5.

Healy, L. (2007) 'Universalism and cultural relativism in social work ethics', *International Social Work*, 50(1): 11–26.

Held, V. (2007) *The Ethics of Care: Personal, Political, Global*. Oxford: Oxford University Press.

Holland, T. (1989) 'Values, faith and professional practice', *Social Thought*, 15(1): 29–41.

Horne, M. (1999) *Values in Social Work*, 2nd edn. Aldershot: Ashgate Arena.

Hudson, B. and Henwood, M. (2008) *Prevention, Personalisation and Prioritisation in Social Care: Squaring the Circle?* London: Commission for Social Care Inspection. Available at: www.melaniehenwood.com/documents/CSCI_FACS_Squaring_the_Circle.pdf (accessed January 2012).

Hudson, M. (1995) *Managing without Profit: The Art of Managing Third Sector Organizations*. Harmondsworth: Penguin.

Hume, D. (2007 [1739]) *A Treatise of Human Nature*. Sioux Falls, SD: Nuvision.

Humphrey, C. (2009) 'The faith closet', *Journal of Practice Teaching and Learning*, 8(3): 7–27.

Humphries, B. (2004) 'An unacceptable role for social work: implementing immigration policy', *British Journal of Social Work*, 34(1): 93–107.

International Federation of Social Workers (IFSW) (2004) *Ethics in Social Work: Statement of Principles*. Available at: www.ifsw.org/cm_data/Ethics_in_Social_Work_Statement_of_Principles_-_to_be_publ_205.pdf (accessed May 2011).

Jefferson, T. (1776) *Declaration of Independence*. Available at: www.archives.gov/exhibits/charters/declaration_transcript.html (accessed 16 June 2012).

Jordan, B. (1991) 'Competencies and values', *Social Work Education*, 10(1): 5–11.

Kalish, R.A. and Reynolds, D.K. (1976) *Death and Ethnicity: A Psychocultural Study*. Los Angeles, CA: University of Southern California Press.

Keating, F. (1997) *Developing an Integrated Approach to Oppression*. London: CCETSW.

Kinney, M. (2009) 'Being assessed under the 1983 Mental Health Act: can it ever be ethical?', *Ethics and Social Welfare*, 3(3): 329–36.

Koggel, C. and Orme, J. (2010) 'Care ethics: new theories and applications' (editorial), *Ethics and Social Welfare*, 4(2): 109–14.

Laming, Lord H. (2003) *Report of an Inquiry into the Death of Victoria Climbié*. London: TSO.

Leadbetter, D. (2004) *Personalisation through Participation: A New Script for Public Services*. London: Demos.

Levy, B. (2003) 'Mind matters: cognitive and physical effects of aging self-stereotypes', *Journal of Gerontology*, 58B(4): 203–11.

Lewis, J. and Glennerster, H. (1996) *Implementing the New Community Care*. Buckingham: Open University Press.

McCaffrey, T. (1998) 'The pain of managing', in A. Foster and V. Zagier Roberts (eds) *Managing Mental Health in the Community*. London: Routledge, pp. 97–107.

McLaren, M. (2007) 'Exploring the ethics of forewarning: social workers, confidentiality and potential child abuse disclosures', *Ethics and Social Welfare*, 1(1): 22–40.

McLaughlin, K. (2008) *Social Work, Politics and Society*. Bristol: Policy Press.

Macnicol, J. (2006) *Age Discrimination: A Historical and Contemporary Analysis*. Cambridge: Cambridge University Press.

Macpherson, W. (1999) *The Stephen Lawrence Enquiry: Report of an Inquest*. London: TSO.

Mandela, N. (1994) *Long Walk to Freedom*. London: Abacus.

Margolin, L. (1997) *Under the Cover of Kindness: The Invention of Social Work*. Charlottesville, VA: University of Virginia Press.

Marx, K. and Engels, F. (2004 [1848]) *The Communist Manifesto*. London: Penguin.

Mercer, G. (2002) 'Disability and oppression: changing theories and practices', in D. Tomlinson and W. Trew (eds) *Equalising Opportunities, Minimising Oppression: A Critical Review of Anti-discriminatory Policies in Health and Social Welfare*. London: Routledge, pp. 117–33.

Moss, B. (2005) *Religion and Spirituality*. Lyme Regis: Russell House.

Moss, B. (2008) 'Pushing back the boundaries: the challenge of spirituality for practice teaching', *Journal of Practice Teaching in Health and Social Work*, 8(3): 48–64.

Munro, E. (2007) 'Confidentiality in a preventative child welfare system', *Ethics and Social Welfare*, 1(1): 41–55.

Munro, E. (2008) *Effective Child Protection*, 2nd edn. London: Sage.

Munro, E. (2011) *The Munro Review of Child Protection. Final Report: A Child-centred System*. London: Department for Education. Available at: www.education.gov.uk/munro review/downloads/8875_DfE_Munro_Report_TAGGED.pdf (accessed May 2011).

National Association of Social Workers (NASW) (2008) *Code of Ethics of the National Association of Social Workers*. Available at: www.naswdc.org/pubs/code/code.asp (accessed October 2011).

Nicholson, R. (1995) *Rumi: Poet and Mystic*. Oxford: Oneworld.

Norman, R. (1998) *The Moral Philosophers: An Introduction to Ethics*, 2nd edn. Oxford: Oxford University Press.

Oakley, J. and Cocking, D. (2001) *Virtue Ethics and Professional Roles*. Cambridge: Cambridge University Press.

O'Beirne, M. (2004) *Religion in England and Wales: Findings from the 2001 Home Office Citizenship Survey*. London: Home Office. Available at www.mssl.ucl.ac.uk/~rs1/hors274. pdf (accessed July 2011).

Olsen, J., Richardson, J., Dolan, P. and Menzel, P. (2003) 'The moral relevance of personal characteristics in setting healthcare priorities', *Social Science and Medicine*, 57(7): 1163–72.

Orwell, G. (2004 [1949]) *Nineteen Eighty-Four*. Harmondsworth: Penguin.

Ovretveit, J. (1998) *Evaluating Health Interventions*. Buckingham: Open University Press.

Oxford Dictionary of English (2009) *ODE*, 2nd edn. Oxford: Oxford University Press.

Parrott, L. (2010) *Values and Ethics in Social Work Practice*, 2nd edn. Exeter: Learning Matters.

Payne, G. (2006) 'An introduction to "social divisions"', in G. Payne (ed.) *Social Divisions*, 2nd edn. Basingstoke: Palgrave, pp. 3–22.

Pease, B. (2009) 'From radical to critical social work: progressive transformation or mainstream incorporation?', in R. Adams, L. Dominelli and M. Payne (eds) *Critical Practice in Social Work*, 2nd edn. Basingstoke: Palgrave, pp. 189–98.

Perry, R. and Cree, V. (2003) 'The changing gender profile of applicants to qualifying social work training in the UK', *Social Work Education*, 22(4): 375–83.

Philpot, T. (1986) *Social Work: A Christian Perspective*. Hertford: Lion Publishing.

Proudhon, P-J. (1994) *What is Property?* (edited by Kelley, D. and Smith, B.) Cambridge: Cambridge University Press.

Raban, J. (2003) 'The greatest gulf', *The Guardian*, 19 April. Available at: www.guardian. co.uk/books/2003/apr/19/iraq.politics (accessed July 2011).

Rachels, J. (1999) *The Elements of Moral Philosophy*, 3rd edn. Boston, MA: McGraw Hill.

Rogers, C. (1967) *On Becoming a Person: A Therapist's View of Psychotherapy*. London: Constable & Robinson.

Schön, D. (1991) *The Reflective Practitioner: How Professionals Think in Action*. Aldershot: Arena.

Scott, J. (2006) 'Class and stratification', in G. Payne (ed.) *Social Divisions*, 2nd edn. Basingstoke: Palgrave, pp. 25–62.

Scourfield, P. (2007) 'Social care and the modern citizen: client, consumer, service user, manager and entrepreneur', *British Journal of Social Work*, 37(1): 107–22.

Shakespeare, T. (2010) 'The cruel toll of disability hate crime', *The Guardian*, 12 March. Available at: www.guardian.co.uk/commentisfree/2010/mar/12/disability-hate-crime-david-askew (accessed February 2012).

Sheppard, M. (2006) *Social Work and Social Exclusion: The Idea of Practice*. Aldershot: Ashgate.

Sheppard, M. with Kelly, N. (2001) *Social Work with Depressed Mothers in Child and Family Care*. London: TSO.

Shor, R. (2000) 'Child maltreatment: differences in perceptions between parents in low income and middle income neighbourhoods', *British Journal of Social Work*, 30: 165–78.

Sibeon, R. (1991) *Towards a New Sociology of Social Work*. Avebury: Aldershot.

Silavwe, G. (1995) 'The need for a new social work perspective in an African setting: the case of social casework in Zambia', *British Journal of Social Work*, 25(1): 71–84.

Smith, R. (2008) *Social Work and Power*. Basingstoke: Palgrave.

Sollod, R. (1992) 'The hollow curriculum: the place of religion and spirituality in society is too often missing', *The Chronicle of Higher Education*, 38(28): 60.

Soyer, D. (1963) 'The right to fail', *Social Work*, 8(3): 72–8.

Spicker, P. (1990) 'Social work and self-determination', *British Journal of Social Work*, 20(3): 221–36.

Svensson, K. (2009) 'Identity work through support and control', *Ethics and Social Welfare*, 3(3): 234–48.

Tanner, D. and Harris, J. (2008) *Working with Older People*. London: Routledge.

Taylor, H., Beckett, C. and McKeigue, B. (2008) 'Judgements of Solomon: anxieties and defences of social workers involved in care proceedings', *Child and Family Social Work*, 13(1): 23–31.

Thoburn, J. (1995) *Paternalism or Partnership*. London: TSO.

Thompson, N. (2006) *Anti-discriminatory Practice*, 4th edn. Basingstoke: Palgrave.

Thompson, S. (2005) *Age Discrimination*. Lyme Regis: Russell House Publishing.

Trevithick, P. (2000) *Social Work Skills: A Practice Handbook*. Buckingham: Open University Press.

Walker, S. and Beckett, C. (2010) *Social Work Assessment and Intervention*, 2nd edn. Lyme Regis: Russell House.

Wilding, P. (1982) *Professional Power and Social Welfare*. London: Routledge & Kegan Paul.

Wilson, A. and Beresford, P. (2000) '"Anti-oppressive practice": emancipation or appropriation?', *British Journal of Social Work*, 30(5): 553–73.

Wintour, P. (2011) 'David Cameron tells Muslim Britain: stop tolerating extremists', *The Guardian*, 5 February. Available at: www.guardian.co.uk/politics/2011/feb/05/david-cameron-muslim-extremism (accessed February 2011).

INDEX